How to Be a
Dog Psychic

How to Be a
Dog Psychic

LEARN TO COMMUNICATE
WITH YOUR PET

Danika Nadzan

FAIR WINDS
PRESS
GLOUCESTER, MASSACHUSETTS

Text © 2005 by Danika Nadzan

First published in the USA in 2005 by
Fair Winds Press, a member of
Quayside Publishing Group
33 Commercial Street
Gloucester, MA 01930

09 08 07 06 05 1 2 3 4 5

ISBN 1-59233-103-3

Library of Congress Cataloging-in-Publication Data available

Cover design by Ariana Grabec-Dingman
Book design by Laura H. Couallier, Laura Herrmann Design

Printed and bound in USA

*The information in this book is for educational purposes only.
It is not intended to replace the advice of a veterinarian. Please see your veterinarian before beginning any new health program for your dog.*

To
my Pretty Girl
and
all the animals who have added
so much to my life.

Acknowledgments

A book is never written by the author alone; there are many contributors to the finished work, and my book is no different. While I'm not able to thank each and every one who helped me to write this book, I acknowledge their contributions all the same.

My parents raised me with an open mind and an open heart, and for this I am forever grateful. The many people who have continued to support me along my sometimes eccentric path through life also deserve acknowledgment—you know who you are—thanks for sticking with me! My husband, Jim, has put up with my long hours in front of the computer over the last six months and has continued to encourage me along the way. (And kept me and the household going!) He's also been a great PR person! Cindy Wenger has been a good friend and animal communication colleague from our first class together. I am grateful for her kind support and friendship.

Everyone at Fair Winds Press has been great and I especially thank my editor, Ellen Phillips, for approaching me with the opportunity to do this book. Her enthusiasm for her work is inspiring, and her encouragement has helped bring one of my dreams to fruition. I hope we can work together again!

And finally, I'm thankful for all the animals in my life and my animal communication clients. They have entrusted me with their thoughts, feelings, and problems, and over the years I've been privy to many very private moments between pets and their families. I hope that I have lived up to their trust, and that I've helped to improve their lives by providing a connection between the species. My greatest hope is that this book will help many others build better and stronger connections among all species, and that in the end, we will see that we are part of one big family.

For all my relations, Peace,
Danika Nadzan, July 2005

Table of Contents

How I Learned to Talk to Dogs—and You Can, Too!

If there was something in the air

If there was something in the wind

If there was something in the trees or bushes

That could be pronounced and once was overheard by animals,

Let this Sacred Knowledge be returned to us again.

—Atharva Veda

When I was a child, my favorite stories were about animals who could talk and about people who could talk to animals. I loved *Charlotte's Web,* E.B. White's classic children's book, and the *Dr. Dolittle* movie. Like many other children, I often talked to my "zoo" of stuffed animals, pets, and even wild animals, telling them all of my secrets and troubles. It was comforting to have such devoted listeners, and I was certain that they understood me and returned my feelings—it seemed only natural.

At the time, movies, television shows, and books about the paranormal—such as *The Twilight Zone, Bewitched, 2001: A Space Odyssey,* and *Mary Poppins*—were very popular. Some abilities, such as extra-sensory perception (or ESP, as it was commonly known), were discussed in popular magazines and became acceptable as subjects of scientific investigation.

I was fortunate to grow up in a family where unusual abilities were not only assumed to be possible but considered within the realm of normal behavior. For instance, my mom was able to "tell" my dad to pick up a specific kind of ice cream on his way home from work. At that time, we had only one family car, and there were no cell phones. I still remember one afternoon when my mom realized that it was a few minutes past 5:00 p.m. and she had forgotten to call my dad at work. She stood by the phone and said out loud, "Bud, bring home cherry-vanilla ice cream," several times. About half an hour later, Dad showed up, carrying the requested half-gallon, claiming that "for some reason" he just thought he'd stop for ice cream on the way home. When Mom told him of her message to him, we all laughed. It was not the first time her message had gotten through.

Mom also believed that everything had feelings, from stuffed animals to teacups to trees to cars—our old family station wagon

Mark This Spot!

Throughout my life, books about animals and people's interactions with them have comprised a large percentage of my reading, and I'm not sure whether those choices resulted from my love of animals or contributed to it. As a preteen, I absolutely loved *The Black Stallion* series by Walter Farley (and, later, the beautiful movie version). When I was a teenager, *Hanta Yo* by Ruth Beebe Hill greatly influenced my life with its insider's perspective on the daily life and spirituality of the Lakota people and their close connection with animals.

In my twenties, I gravitated to photographer Jim Brandenburg's *Brother Wolf* and found kindred spirits in the author and his subjects. A friend introduced me to *The Education of Little Tree* by Forrest Carter, which reaffirmed my admiration for the way of life of the indigenous peoples of the Americas.

In my thirties, I made *Travels with Charley* by John Steinbeck a companion on my yearly vacations, wishing as I read that I had stowed away with the author and his witty blue poodle. Another friend gave me a copy of *Urban Shaman* by Serge Kahili King, PhD, and it opened a whole new world for me with simple exercises (which I will explain later in this book) that made huge changes in my life.

I recommend that you read some of these favorites, and I'll recommend others as we go along. They'll enrich your understanding of animals—as well as your psychic abilities.

even was named Nelly. Because of my mother's belief, I learned to respect and appreciate everything that came into my life.

My dad had an insatiable curiosity and rarely said that anything was impossible, even though his engineering background told him that it might be improbable. In fact, we constantly were reminded that "I can't" was not an acceptable response to anything. His mind was open enough to accept the possibility of things, and he handed that down to me.

The combination of attitudes that my parents fostered no doubt greatly affected how I viewed the natural world and my relationship to it. In my teenage years, I was drawn to Native American and Eastern spiritual beliefs and felt a deep connection with the view that all things had spirits. The idea that *anything* could be a teacher resonated with me. It encouraged me to become an avid observer of and listener to other creatures.

FIRST PSYCHIC STEPS

As I continued on my spiritual journey, I began to find that creatures would respond to my requests when I expressed them respectfully. For example, I once had a colony of sugar ants trooping daily into my kitchen and across my countertop to reach my cupboard. Although I didn't want the ants in my food, I had no desire to kill them, either. One honey jar in the cabinet was almost empty, so I stood quietly at the kitchen sink one day and spoke to the ants in my thoughts. "I understand that you are just trying to find food, but this is my house. I have no wish to harm you, but I will have no choice if you continue to invade my food supplies. Please work with me. You can have the honey jar but nothing else in the cabinet. If I see you in any other food, I will have to do something drastic."

The next day and for several days thereafter, in the early morning I saw a single line of ants marching across the countertop, up to the cabinet, and into the honey jar. The jar was black with ants, but no other foodstuff was infested. The ants had accepted my bargain!

When the honey jar was completely clean, the ants stopped coming, except for a few scouts. After that, I would put nearly empty jelly jars or syrup bottles just outside the back door where the colony had entered, and they stopped coming into the house altogether. Needless to say, I was amazed.

Some time later, I had a problem with my female cat, Tuxedo, not using the litter box. The situation was extremely distressing and smelly, and I was at my wits' end trying to find a suitable solution to the problem. Because I was so distraught, I did not think to have a calm conversation with Tuxedo. It's funny that I thought to speak to "strange" ants but not to my beloved house companion. In any case, I was prodded into action when a book about animal communication (most professionals prefer to be called "animal communicators" rather than "pet psychics") literally jumped off a shelf in front of me when I was visiting a book store. I had never heard the term "animal communication" used to describe what I did, and I was curious to read about someone else's experience with it.

The book gave me the nudge I needed, and after a 15-minute discussion with Tuxy, I learned that the "boys" (my three male cats, who also shared the household) were tormenting her. Every time she used the covered litter box, one of them would lie in wait just outside it and pounce on her as she exited. She was surprised and terrified each time, so she finally decided not to use the box. They also terrorized her at night after I went to bed, waiting for her to fall asleep and then leaping on her. When I asked her how I could fix the situation, she told me that taking the cover off the box would help, and that she would like to sleep in a "safe spot." I got rid of the cover and gave her a comfy bed in a spare bedroom, where I closed the door each night (providing her with her own private litter box, of course). Although there were still occasional mishaps, life quickly got better for both of us.

I also had a conversation with the mischievous boys. During our conversations, I discovered that the real culprits were Merlin and Pine. Both of them confessed to their deeds, but neither was very recalcitrant. In fact, they behaved not unlike many human brothers: They thought teasing and surprising Tuxy was great fun, and they thought she should lighten up. Over the years, I repeatedly have asked for their cooperation, but to this day, they still find it hard to pass up an opportunity to startle her. I honestly believe that the temptation of a guaranteed reaction is too much to resist, and I have to say that there are times when she seems to provoke the attention. Like I said, it seems similar to some family interactions I know.

After that situation with the household felines, I discovered that there were workshops available that could help me hone my skills and where I could learn how to be a professional animal communicator. The thought of helping animals in need definitely appealed to me, and learning from two well-known communicators seemed a wise choice. The workshop setting was fun and invaluable because it enabled me to validate my skills further by doing exercises with complete strangers and their animals and getting immediate feedback. Talking to someone else's pet and receiving information you couldn't possibly know—and that is so detailed and specific that it generates an "Ohmigod!" response from the person—does wonders for your confidence.

MY LIFE AS AN ANIMAL COMMUNICATOR

I completed workshops with renowned animal communicators Penelope Smith and Anita Curtis and took a follow-up course on becoming a professional communicator. Then I began taking phone calls from people who needed help with their companion animals, and have been doing so now for about ten years. I also do readings in person, appear at expos and fairs with another communicator friend, Cindy Wenger, and hope to branch out to work with animal rescue groups.

Along the way, I have found that I have a special gift for discerning medical issues, which I may have inherited from my grandmother, who was a practical nurse and reflexologist. Happily, I have saved some lives because of it. This part of my ability sometimes manifests itself without any conscious effort on my part and without even a request by others. There's a story in Chapter 6 about one particular instance in which a Lhasa apso rather forcefully indicated her problem to me, even though the owner had not asked me to talk to her. Fortunately, I was with a group of fairly open-minded people who knew that I communicated with animals, and they realized that the message I blurted out was urgent. The woman later confirmed the information, and the dog eventually recovered completely. Episodes like this continually remind me that animal communication is a worthwhile skill to develop and use.

It's important to note here that I *never* provide animal-communication services as a replacement for veterinary care. I only aid pet owners with information from the animal that may help the veterinarian diagnose or treat an ailment. I am not a veterinarian, and I do not have any schooling in medicine—I simply allow the animal to tell me what he or she feels or knows. Sometimes I am able to scan an animal and describe an ailment in human terms, making it easier to suggest an area to check—for example, I've felt a chronic pain coupled with a mental image of a sort of "Swiss cheese" effect that turned out to be cancer. This information may give a veterinarian a place to start checking for a problem.

I do recommend some caution in how you relay information to your vet. Although many pet owners are quite open to the idea of animal communication, I find that veterinarians are slower to accept it. Some, especially those who work with horses, seem to welcome the extra input, but others will tell you flat out that animals can't talk. So think before you go running to your vet's office and declare that an animal communicator told you what's wrong with your dog —the whole idea is to help vets not infuriate them. I believe that as more people learn to communicate and get good results, more veterinarians will see it as just another tool to help them help animals.

You Can Do It!

I know through my own development and training that our ability to communicate telepathically is not a special talent. We all have the ability to transmit telepathic messages, but most of us have been socialized out of it. Many children converse with the natural world or with their "invisible" friends as a matter of course, until they're told enough times that such things are not possible or generally acceptable. There are some indications that our preverbal human ancestors used telepathy to communicate, but once they were able to speak, the need for telepathy disappeared, and the ability waned. The purpose of this book is to show you that *anyone* can develop the skill to communicate telepathically. In fact, communicating with animals is in some ways much easier than communicating with humans, because animals' minds are not so crowded with day-to-day concerns.

At the core of my beliefs is a realization that everything is connected to everything else, and that this connection makes up the One. Every plant, rock, creature, and substance is, in some way, a reflection of a part of the Divine. I believe that this connectedness is what makes telepathic communication possible. It also is why such things as dowsing and spiritual journeying, discussed later in this book, can provide answers—because at the very center of our beings, we are connected to the One who has all the answers. These things are not "magic," except to those who have forgotten their connection. My intent is to reopen your lines of communication with our siblings in the Universe and to help you recognize the rest of your family so that we may all live together in peace.

Over the course of my communications, I have met many wonderful people and animals and continue to be amazed at the love that people show for their pets, at the animals' capacity for unconditional love, and at how much the animals have to teach us.

The nonhuman beings with whom we share this planet *can* talk to us—in fact, they are just waiting for the opportunity to have a conversation. It is we humans who need to accept that they have something to say. Then we must develop the fine art of *communication,* which, by definition, implies a two-way transfer of information. We've already spent centuries expecting our animal friends to become bilingual so we can tell them what to do. Now it's our turn—to listen. When we do, life only can get better.

Please note that the names of pets and people used in the examples throughout this book have been changed, except where full names are used, to protect the privacy of the individuals.

The
Psychic Link

He is your friend, your partner, your defender, your dog. You are his life, his love, his leader. He will be yours, faithful and true, to the last beat of his heart. You owe it to him to be worthy of such devotion.

—Unknown

Anyone who ever has had the privilege of living with a dog knows what it feels like to be loved unconditionally. These soulful beings often embody the qualities we adored in our favorite childhood stuffed animals—they're good listeners, they're always eager to play, and, when we're down or sick, they're right there to comfort us. Unfortunately, sometimes we unintentionally treat them like stuffed animals—easily accessible when we want them and just as easily put away when we don't.

On the other hand, at times even the sweetest pup can be like a toddler in the midst of "the terrible twos"—demanding, obstinate, and aggravating. Frustrated and guilt-ridden dog owners often think, "If only there was *some* way of understanding what they're thinking!" Well, there is a way, and it's easier than you think. In this book, I'll show you how you too can understand your pup, adolescent, adult, or older dog—and anybody else's as well. We'll begin developing those skills in Chapter 2, Enhancing Your Intuition. But first, let's explore how our psychic link with dogs began and how we finally rediscovered our ability to communicate with our beloved pets in the past few decades.

IN THE BEGINNING

The howling of a wolf on a moonlit night might sound lonely to some, and perhaps in a way that is what drew canines and humans together: a mutual need for companionship. Although there is no record of the first interaction between wolves and humans, the relationship clearly has been developing for a very long time.

Domesticated dogs have been part of human life for at least 10,000 to 12,000 years, as documented by discoveries of human and canine skeletons buried together in a ceremonial fashion. These discoveries make it probable that this association goes back even further: some archeologists now believe our first attempt at cooperation with another predator occurred 100,000 years ago.

At some point in our distant past, wolves and humans were top predators in overlapping territories all over the world. Our species shared many traits, such as high levels of intelligence, similar dietary preferences, comparable hunting skills, and organized social behavior that included close-knit family units. Early humans and wolves probably did not fear each other—top-level predators rarely waste energy attacking each other, because hunting prey is more beneficial and less dangerous—but they probably crossed paths often enough to benefit from watching each other and learning different hunting techniques. And, of course, there were bound to be other interactions.

On one day, perhaps humans who lost track of a wounded prey animal would find that wolves had caught up to it and eaten it; on another, wolves who couldn't eat or cache all they killed would return later to find that humans had taken the remains. Because both species clearly had the intelligence and the need to find the easiest way to provide for their families, it made sense to cooperate and share skills. At some point, one side attempted a real communication about joining forces, and it was well received by the other.

The common bond between our species continued to grow through the years, no doubt spurred on by our similarities and mutual objectives. Eventually, some of the wolves chose to live with us permanently, perhaps enjoying the camaraderie between the species.

However, although the wolf apparently was seen as an equal in the beginning, in the long run, humans changed the equation and began to "domesticate" our wild brothers, which is to say *dominate* them. Those wolves who joined us did so at a cost—they gained a certain type of security, but they lost their freedom.

Mark This Spot!

For some excellent insight into the similarities between wolves and humans and how we came to live together, I highly recommend *Brother Wolf: A Forgotten Promise,* by renowned wildlife photographer Jim Brandenburg. Brandenburg spent years following and studying a pack of wolves that live on his property in Minnesota, and his love and admiration for them compelled him to write this book. The combination of his breathtaking photographs and his well-written and well-researched text will give you a completely new understanding not just of wolves but also of those just-this-side-of-wild canines who live with us.

When Wolf Became Dog

Over time, through continuous manipulation by humans, the wolf became the domestic dog, in all its astonishing variations. Note that although there are distinct differences in the DNA of wolves, coyotes, foxes, and jackals, the genetic difference between wolves and dogs is so small that their DNA is virtually indistinguishable. In fact, some archeologists find that skull differences are more accurate indicators of genetic differences than DNA is. This close connection may explain why, even after all this time, there still is a wildness in our canine companions that responds to that lonesome howl on a summer's evening. In a bizarre way, this human–canine collaboration also has secured the genetic future of the wolf. At present, many varieties of wild wolves are endangered species, yet there are approximately 65 million pet dogs in the United States alone.

From observation of their traits and behaviors, our ancestors found that wolves knew instinctively how to live as part of a group. Through their willingness to participate in human life and activities, coupled with their intelligence and physical prowess, wolves enabled humans to reach high levels of accomplishment much more quickly than we would have on our own.

For example, just having a partner with much greater speed, stamina, and physical strength to track and kill prey meant that fewer humans were needed to hunt, fewer died in the process, and more food was brought back to the family. Having a guard with far more sensitive senses of smell, hearing, and sight provided an early warning system that undoubtedly saved many lives. And the willingness of the wolves/dogs to work as pack animals greatly increased humans' ability to cover larger areas of land for a wider variety of purposes—not just hunting.

Thus, when *Canis lupis,* the wolf, became *Canis familiaris,* the dog, the association allowed human civilization to begin taking large technological leaps. Better hunt results meant more stable food supplies, which meant less need for a nomadic existence. This in turn meant more time for other pursuits, which led to agriculture and domestication of prey animals, and the dog became a herding assistant, guard, and transport. Increased supplies resulted in trade and further expansion of human technology. Indeed, it's quite possible that humans made it to the top of the food chain by climbing on the dog's back.

REDISCOVERING THE PSYCHIC LINK

This close, long-term association of human and dog has no doubt contributed to the psychic bond between us. Perhaps because of their behavioral similarities to us, dogs understand and relate to humans better than any other animal does. By virtue of their natural ability to read facial expressions and body language, as well as to communicate telepathically, dogs have learned to understand us much better than we understand them.

By welcoming dogs into our families and sharing our daily lives with them, however, we have increased our need to communicate with them. The ability to talk to nonhuman beings has been used for centuries and is seen as normal by many cultures on the planet, especially those that are closely connected to animals, such as hunter-gatherers. However, people in the industrialized West only recently started to admit that it is possible to "talk" to animals and have them "talk" back. For centuries, those educated in the Western sciences have accepted as fact the idea that animals have no feelings, thoughts, or souls.

This belief is, of course, very handy when much of your cultural identity is predicated upon the belief that humans were made to dominate the Earth and all its inhabitants. It becomes much more difficult to justify using and abusing other creatures and their habitats if you think of them as sentient beings with intellects and spirits and purposes of their own. I feel that this interest in renewing our ability to communicate with animals indicates that there are many of us who now are ready to return to our place in the natural world—as part of the whole instead of separate from it.

In the late nineteenth and early twentieth centuries in the West, there began a slow return from a long detour away from the natural world. People started speaking out against the cruel treatment of animals and began to form humane societies to put their beliefs into action. Well-known men of science, such as Albert Schweitzer and Albert Einstein, voiced their belief that reverence for all life was normal and natural—and that, as humans, we were only part of Creation, not necessarily the pinnacle or it.

In 1954, J. Allen Boone wrote a book, *Kinship with All Life,* in which he explored this connectedness. His amazing relationship with Strongheart, a very special German shepherd, started him on the road to animal communication and eventually led him to write this and other classic volumes. Later, in the 1960s and 1970s, a cultural revolution was taking place in the United States, and those in the scientific community were urged to stretch their imaginations further, widening the bounds of what science considered "real." Abilities other than those generally accepted as normal were now at least being investigated as "extra-sensory" or "paranormal" possibilities.

Even the governments of the Western world began to acknowledge that psychic abilities might be real, from the remote viewers who helped locate enemy targets during World War II to President Reagan's astrologer in the 1980s. The public's interest continued to grow as more books, movies, and television shows focused on all things supernatural. From "the Force" in *Star Wars* to *The X-Files* television show, the "paranormal" was on its way to becoming just "normal."

Dr. Sheldrake and Scientific Acceptance

Also during this time, biologist and biochemist Rupert Sheldrake, PhD, published his revolutionary hypothesis of morphic resonance, the idea that Nature itself has memory that influences the current forms and behaviors of organisms. According to this hypothesis, morphic resonance causes baby humans to look like humans and causes puppies to look like dogs. It also is a sort of "species consciousness," which explains, among other things, Sheldrake's findings that once a certain number of animals have learned a specific thing, others of the same species either will automatically know it or will learn it more easily.

Sheldrake continued to challenge the deep-seated assumptions of modern science in the 1990s with two books that investigated unexplained phenomena and the psychic abilities of pets, *Seven Experiments That Could Change the World: A Do-It-Yourself Guide to Revolutionary Science* and *Dogs That Know When Their Owners Are Coming Home, and Other Unexplained Powers of Animals*. The second book won the 1999 Book of the Year Award from the British Scientific and Medical Network. Both books brought into question the existing paradigms of scientific thought regarding such controversial subjects, which in the past had been proclaimed "impossible to prove" and then simply ignored. Sheldrake provided simple experiments to show that these phenomena exist and documented the results. Even today, he continues to encourage the general public to contribute to his ongoing research.

Dogs That Know When Their Owners Are Coming Home is particularly relevant for animal communicators. In it, Dr. Sheldrake directly addresses the subject of human–animal telepathy, and the entire book is about the experiments he conducted and the results that appear to support the theory that it does exist. Probably the most important thing about Sheldrake's work, however, is that he is a well-respected scientist with a history of solid scientific research.

Although his ideas may be seen as outside the mainstream, he is well aware of this perception and strives to follow standard scientific research procedures. By doing so, he has produced a body of evidence that supports his theories—and he does not stop there. He welcomes other scientists' viewpoints and encourages them to devise experiments to support their own theories or to disprove his. He also encourages the general public to get involved in the scientific debate by making his experiments easy to perform and document and by providing a Web site for sharing data and building a database.

Mark This Spot!

You may want to investigate Rupert Sheldrake's work and try some of his experiments yourself. Read his book, *Dogs That Know When Their Owners Are Coming Home and Other Unexplained Powers of Animals,* and check out his Web site at **www.sheldrake.org**.

PROFESSIONAL ANIMAL COMMUNICATORS

During the late 1980s and into the 1990s, animal communication began to gain widespread acceptance when professionals such as Penelope Smith, Jeri Ryan, Anita Curtis, and Carole Devereux began teaching others, through books and workshops, to reawaken their ability to talk with the animals. Then, in June of 2002, *The Pet Psychic* television show made its debut on the Animal Planet cable channel, and British-born communicator Sonya Fitzpatrick brought animal communication to the masses. Today, there are thousands of animal communicators, several professional organizations, and dozens of classes and workshops offered every year for people eager to expand their ability to communicate with animals. See the Resources section beginning on page 198 for more information about them.

Many of the wild creatures who have spoken through communicators have messages of hope for our return to unity with them. They are anxious to speak with humans and have much information and insight to share with us, if only we will open our hearts and minds and *listen.*

My hope is that this book will help you to reawaken your ability to communicate with animals and that it will help you and your dog have a better life together. I also hope that you will use your skills to expand your experience of the natural world by conversing with the many other beings with whom we share this wonderful planet. We have so much to learn!

Let's get started in the next chapter with exercises that will help you enhance your intuitive skills—the first step toward being able to talk to your dog and hear what he or she is saying in return.

Enhancing Your Intuition

"So we're having a dinner party, and everyone is standing around chatting, enjoying their drinks before dinner. Ollie (the English sheepdog) is happily mixing among the guests, behaving himself, and lapping up anything that hits the floor. Everything's going along fine, but about half an hour later I notice I'm feeling very cramped—it's like the walls have moved in by several feet. No one else seems to notice, but I glance around the room and realize what's happened: Ollie has quietly and methodically herded the crowd into a corner! I guess I forgot to tell him he was 'off duty' for the night!"

—Diane B.

Has your pup ever cocked his head at specific words, recognizing your intent to hand out a treat or go for a ride? Have you ever just *known* that the roguish imp completely understands you but is pretending not to hear? And what dog owner hasn't seen that look that just begs forgiveness after your dog has committed a transgression? Who wouldn't want to know exactly what's going on behind those limpid, loving, mischievous eyes?

The first step in learning telepathic animal communication is simply believing that it is possible. The fact that you're reading this book probably is a good indication that you're ready to do so.

Most people who live with dogs already know that they have feelings. It's not difficult to recognize when a dog is happy, angry, or uncomfortable: the wagging tail, growling, or whining and whimpering are easy-to-understand displays of emotion. Contrary to what some scientists still try to tell us, dogs are not automatons reacting solely to external stimuli in a genetically prescribed fashion. Anyone who's had canine companions knows that what makes one dog happy or angry does not necessarily affect another dog in the same way.

Doggie Diaries

I've learned that dogs try to communicate with us all the time, but often we don't listen until they do something drastic. For example, my mom's dog, Scruffy, an aptly named terrier-husky mix, was extremely intelligent and had a repertoire of barks with different meanings that in some cases sounded like words. Scruffy, after having stood at the back door and barked "Out!" several times, finally lost patience with my mother's delay in rousing herself from the recliner.

In a last-ditch effort to get her to understand his urgency, he walked into the dining room and, within her sight, made a show of ever-so-gently grasping in his teeth a single leaf of her favorite houseplant. He was obviously threatening more serious damage if she continued to ignore his request. My mom immediately got the message and got up to let him out, and the plant was not harmed.

—Marie N.

Learning to Trust Our Intuition

There's a look of recognition that comes over a dog's face when she completely understands what's expected or anticipated. Words such as "food," "treat," "walk," or "ride" are most likely among the words that trigger such a look. But recognition also occurs at times when you haven't even spoken a word. Have you ever tried to pack for a trip without your dog's constant intervention? Have you ever thought about an upcoming visit to the veterinarian and then spent thirty minutes playing hide-and-seek with your suddenly disappearing dog? Or do ever wonder how they just *know* when today's the day to visit the dog park?

On the human side of this equation, we often have an inkling that something "just isn't right" with our furry family member, even before physical symptoms manifest. Or we may feel a knot in our stomach without knowing why, even before we look in the backyard and realize that someone left the gate open.

We've all heard the term "gut feeling" to describe an information source that seems to have little connection to what we consider to be normal sensory data perception. The term itself implies a disconnection from our normal thinking process and more of a connection to our feeling nature. In fact, in defense of an action we may have taken based on this intuition, we might say, "I don't know; I just felt it was the thing to do," or "My gut told me." Not exactly a rational-sounding response, but we've all done it and said it.

In fact, that feeling of *knowing* is real. It is connected to normal sensory data perception; it's just that many of us have neglected this particular sense for so long that it seems strange. Children often accept intuition as normal and often base their actions solely on those gut feelings. They often continue to do so until they are forced by social conditioning to change.

I'd like to help you remember this "sixth sense" and increase your skill in using it. Once you believe that you have the ability, the next step is to extend that belief to include animals. You already know they have feelings, so this step should be easy. After all, if you'd like to have a conversation with your dog, it helps if you believe that he actually has the capacity to form independent thoughts and might be willing to share them with you.

And just a word about speciesism: It's quite natural for humans to believe that they're the pinnacle of creation, but this point of view is subjective. Beware of taking this attitude into the realm of animal communication. Other species value life as much as we do, and they don't necessarily subscribe to the idea that humans are the cream of the crop. (Just ask any cat!) In fact, if you branch out into conversing with animals other than your dog, you may be quite surprised at some of the information and attitudes that you receive, especially from the wild animal kingdom.

What I'm advocating here is an open mind and a reverence for Life—*all* Life. Because no matter how insignificant, ugly, or "useless" you as a human may think it is, each creature's life is important to that creature. Killing something just to kill it is hard to justify after you realize this fact. No matter how tiny and simple something like an ant may appear, you don't have the ability to make another one just like it. When I see someone stomp on a bug and hear them say, "Well, it's just a bug!" I usually respond with, "Fine, then make me another one, since it's so insignificant!" If nothing else, it may get them to think about what they're doing.

Mark This Spot!

To help you expand your respect and consideration for other creatures, especially those who are labeled pests, try reading *Reverence for Life* by Albert Schweitzer, or *Animals Nobody Loves* by Ronald Rood. Dr. Schweitzer's compassion for the animal kingdom is legendary, and this often-quoted essay excellently explains his position. Ronald Rood is a well-known naturalist, and in this book he takes up the cause of a dozen animals whose "worth" (or lack of it) in human terms is based almost entirely upon ignorance. He looks at our myths and misunderstandings and proceeds to enlighten the reader with some of the amazing facts about creatures who rightfully fill a place in creation.

Once you've reacquainted yourself with your telepathic abilities using the exercises in this chapter, try sitting outside somewhere and conversing with whatever creature comes along—I've had wonderful conversations with dragonflies, crickets, birds, and even a housefly or two. And you may find, as I have, that insects often honor your requests when approached respectfully—I no longer have to use mosquito spray, and I've had many spiders crawl right into a cup to be carried outside.

Now we've established a belief that intuition exists, that we all are capable of it, and that by "we all" we mean other creatures as well as ourselves. Let's continue.

Doggie Diaries

I don't consider myself an animal communicator, but it's clear that I have some connection with certain animals. For example, there's an area I drive through regularly that is heavily populated with deer. I mentally ask the deer to stay in the fields and away from my car as I travel through there. At one spot along the way, several deer will stand at the edge of the road just about every night, as if they're waiting for me. I always slow down and stop, allowing them to cross in front of my car. They seem to know that it's me, and that I'll stop and wait for them to safely cross.

—*Cristie S.*

Seven Reasons to Reclaim Your Sixth Sense

Besides the obvious benefit of satisfying curiosity, what are some of the benefits of being able to converse with your dog? Here are seven that spring to mind:

1. ***You'll have peace of mind.*** And I mean both yours and your dog's. For example, think about how much better you'll feel knowing that your dog understands that you only are going to be away for a couple of hours, and that it's not necessary to become nervous and anxious about being alone for too long.

2. ***You'll get early indications of medical problems.*** Having regular conversations with your dog could help you discover when ill health starts, possibly determine some of the probable causes, and provide ample time for early treatment or prevention of more serious illnesses.

3. ***You can correct or prevent behavior problems.*** By communicating your expectations and plans to your dog, you can help him adjust to new situations without the anxiety that causes

many behavior problems. Your dog may not be happy with what you have to say or do, but giving him all the information and an opportunity to provide feedback often will ease tensions before they grow into problems.

4. ***You'll receive helpful feedback.*** You'll be able to know for sure whether your pal wants a companion to play with, or whether the new food tastes good, or whether the doggy day care is worth the money, or how the new baby will be accepted, or just about anything else you can think of.

5. ***You'll develop a stronger relationship.*** Just by allowing your dog to participate in the conversation, you open up a whole new range of relationship possibilities. It's the same way that human-to-human relationships grow—through *communication.* This bond will expand your life in many ways—and also may be extremely helpful in locating your dog if he ever becomes lost.

6. ***You'll gain another perspective.*** Many dogs are excellent therapists—they're good listeners, excellent observers, and naturally honest communicators. Your faithful companion loves you like no one else, and by virtue of the fact that he has seen you at all hours, even at your least appealing, and still loves you anyway, he has a unique authority to offer insights into your nature that others would never know (or wouldn't tell you if they did). Seeing life's difficulties from a canine point of view may reduce those mountains into molehills. (And it won't cost you $200 an hour!)

7. ***You'll learn about your other pets.*** Just as one child will tattle on another, one animal in a multipet household often will gleefully supply all kinds of information about everyone else. Granted, this information sometimes may have to be taken with a grain of salt, but there's usually a good chunk of the truth included in it.

Now that you've got some good reasons to reclaim your talent for communicating with your dog, let's take the next step.

Pawprint

Remember, animal communication is *never* a substitute for proper veterinary care! For your dog's sake, your first responsibility in any medical situation is to check with your vet.

CALMING YOUR MIND

As discussed in Chapter 1, the telepathic abilities of people and animals have been well documented. My purpose here is to give you some simple exercises to help you develop these skills so they will really enhance the experience of living with a canine companion—for you as well as your dog.

The most important part of preparing for telepathic communication is calming your mind. For some people, this task seems to be monumental. Daily lives filled with deadlines, errands, after-school activities, and many other intrusions leave many of us exhausted and unable to focus. These simple exercises not only will prepare you to communicate with your pet but will have the added benefit of giving you a break from your busy day. Practicing visualizations and other forms of meditation is a wonderful way to clear the mind, rejuvenate the spirit, and enhance our ability to connect with others.

Mark This Spot!

Medical studies have shown that the simple act of petting a dog lowers your blood pressure and that pet ownership increases the odds for survival in the case of some serious illnesses—and is even correlated to lower cholesterol and triglyceride levels!

EXERCISE 1

The Sacred Clearing Meditation

This short visualization exercise can be done any time, in about 10 minutes, as a minivacation from the everyday. If you find it difficult to achieve an "empty mind" meditative state, the pleasant imagery used here may be easier for you to work with. Follow these simple steps to reach a more relaxed state of mind:

1. Find a quiet spot where you won't be disturbed.

2. Sit in a relaxed position. If you find it relaxing to sit in the traditional cross-legged lotus position, by all means do so. However, it is not necessary. It's fine to sit in a comfortable upright chair with your feet flat on the floor and your hands either in your lap or resting on your thighs, palms upward.

3. Close your eyes, take a few deep breaths, and, as you exhale, mentally let go of all the distractions of your day.

4. Next, relax your body by first clenching and then releasing each group of muscles consecutively. Start with your feet, then your calves, then your thighs, then your buttocks, abdomen, shoulders, arms, hands, neck, and face.

5. Slowly breathe in and out, listening to the sound of each breath. With your eyes closed, focus on the spot between your eyebrows, known as your "third eye." As your breathing becomes regular, release it from your thought, and let the breath come and go on its own.

6. Picture yourself on a pathway leading through an open, sunny field of brightly colored flowers. The path meanders gently through the waist-high plants, which are gently swaying in the fragrant breeze. Here and there hummingbirds and bees dip gently to drink nectar, and you watch them as you walk along, feeling the warmth of the sun on your arms.

7. As you follow the path, it leads into a forest, where the shade is cool, and you can hear a small brook running nearby. You can see squirrels chasing each other up and down the bark of the huge

trees, and you hear the songs of the woodland birds, crickets, and tree frogs. The sounds and smells of the forest are comforting, and you enjoy listening as you walk along.

8. A little farther along the path you see an archway of light, where the path leads to a clearing. The surrounding trees make the space feel like an outdoor cathedral: sheltered yet open and airy. Near the center of this sacred clearing, there is a group of rounded boulders. As you approach, you can see these are very ancient rocks, well worn by the weather, with interesting marks and colors. When you touch them, they feel warm from the sun, and they are inviting you to sit and rest after your walk.

9. You find a spot to sit, and it is amazingly comfortable; it's as if the rock was molded to fit you. You rest here for a while with your eyes closed, listening to the breeze and the bugs, the birds, and the animals.

10. After a short rest, you open your eyes and look around, taking in every detail of the sacred glade. You know that this is a safe and secure place where you are welcome any time.

11. Now it is time to return, and you amble along the path back through the woods to the open field and back to where you began.

12. Slowly become aware of your breath again, and then return your awareness to your body. Mentally center and ground yourself by feeling the floor beneath your feet. Gently open your eyes and notice how refreshed you feel.

Remember the Sacred Clearing from this exercise—it gives you a safe, secure place in which to do your spiritual work. You can go there any time you need a break or want to work on a specific issue in any aspect of your life. In the future, you may go to this place to prepare yourself to communicate with a dog or other animal or actually to meet animals with whom you wish to communicate. Use it and expand it as you wish; you may find, as I have, that the clearing has other pathways that lead you to other interesting and valuable learning adventures. Go here to expand your vision and to seek answers from within. In the next exercise, we will return to the Sacred Clearing to meet our Spirit Guide.

Pawprint

TIP: Use the sacred clearing as a meeting place for conversations between you and dogs or other animals, birds, insects, or any other beings.

EXERCISE 2

Meet Your Spirit Guide

For many shamans, healers, mediums, and others who do spiritual work, it is essential to have a Spirit Guide who will lead the way and offer advice and protection on the journey into the unknown. A Spirit Guide may be anything: an animal, insect, bird, tree, rock, person, fairy, or angel. It is common to have more than one Spirit Guide. For instance, you may have one guide for animal communication, another for helping with health issues, another for working on career goals, and so on.

Some guides choose you, while others may be people or even fictional characters you select who have traits you admire and wish to emulate. You can ask your guide to come to you in a meditation or even to manifest in the physical world. Sometimes Spirit Guides appear even before you ask!

There was a brief period in my life when everywhere I looked, I saw a butterfly. When I was in the car, one would flit by; when I'd leave my house, one would just be landing on the walkway; if I went to the store, I'd see butterflies on cards, books, or stamps. At one point, I came around a bend and saw a whole field full of them!

When I asked friends if they noticed a preponderance of the creatures, they did not, and one even said, "This message must be for you!" I took it as a sign to pay attention to the butterflies, and so I sat in meditation and asked for any messages they had. I also did a little research about them and read about the meanings that other cultures attributed to them.

It turned out to be a time of great change in my life, and these masters of transformation were offering lessons on living through it with some semblance of grace. After that time, I stopped seeing lots of butterflies, but I know that when I'm heading for change, I always can ask for their guidance again.

Mark This Spot!

In his wonderful book *Urban Shaman,* Serge Kahili King, Ph.D, suggests assembling an Inner Council of Advisors to help you with questions concerning various aspects of your life. He adapted this idea from author Napoleon Hill's technique of using Invisible Counselors, which he explained in his book *Think and Grow Rich.*

The idea is to assemble an imaginary group of helpers with whom you can discuss the various issues of your life to learn new perspectives and ideas that may aid you in solving problems and expanding your creativity. The members can be people you admire, fictional characters, animal or plant spirits, or anything else. Try it—you'll be amazed at how helpful and stress-relieving it is!

Now, to meet your own Spirit Guide, begin the Sacred Clearing visualization you learned in Exercise 1 (see page 37 if you need to review). Sit comfortably, breathe slowly, and follow the same path through the field, through the woods, and to the comfortable resting spot on the warm, ancient rocks.

1. Relax with your eyes closed, listening to the breeze and the music of the creatures around you. Feel the warmth from the rocks beneath you and the sun above you.

2. As you rest there, begin to think about your Spirit Guide. Silently tell your Spirit Guide that you are embarking on a new challenge, and ask your Spirit Guide to visit you here in the Sacred Clearing.

3. After a little while, you will feel a presence beside you; a comfortable feeling of recognition washes over you, even before you open your eyes. The being softly calls your name, and you open your

eyes and look into the face of your Spirit Guide. Silently ask your guide's name, and hear the reply.

4. Explain to your Spirit Guide that you are learning to communicate with animals and would appreciate his or her help. Ask for any guidance or suggestions, and share any concerns or wishes. Then thank your guide for coming to visit you, and say good-bye.

5. Return along the path through the woods, breathing deeply and noticing once again the sights, sounds, and smells of the forest. Go back through the open field, noticing the fragrances of the wild flowers and the sounds of the birds and other flying creatures, and feel the warmth of the sun on your skin.

6. Once you are back where you began, slowly return your awareness to your body. Mentally center and ground yourself by feeling the floor beneath your feet. Gently open your eyes.

Once you have met your Spirit Guide, you may want to find out more about him or her. For example, if your guide is an animal, learn all you can about that animal and its characteristics, habitat, food, and family life. Find out what legends or other cultures say about it. You even may want to have a physical talisman of your guide, such as a carving, necklace, or photo, to remind you of your guide's presence and characteristics.

Mark This Spot!

Author Ted Andrews' book *Animal Speak* is a well-known reference for information on a wide variety of animal guides, including insects, birds, reptiles, and amphibians. It offers lots of insights into the natural world of creatures, as well as their symbolic meanings to various cultures. It's fun to look up all your favorite animals, such as the eagle or bear, or even backyard favorites like the squirrel, as well as your animal guide.

EXERCISE 3

Create a Simple Ritual

This exercise may help you prepare for an animal communication session. Opening your mind and heart is essential to clear communication, and you may find, as I do, that it's easier to do with a small ritual. Performing it is a signal to your mind, heart, and spirit of what you are about to do. A ritual does not have to be magical or mysterious—it's simply a specific set of steps to follow that prepares you to do something. For example, you perform a ritual when you plan a trip to the grocery store or get ready for a night out.

Your assignment for this exercise is to create a simple, pleasant ritual that you can do to calm and center yourself before you attempt to communicate with your dog or another animal. It should be easy to do and easy to remember. Your ritual can be as simple as lighting a candle, sitting in a specific chair, and putting on some meditative background music—anything that signals to you that you are preparing to communicate telepathically is fine.

How to Send and Receive Telepathically

Once you have calmed your mind and opened your heart, you can begin to send and receive messages.

At this point, many people allow their preconceived notions and doubts to overcome their desire to communicate telepathically. It is imperative that you let go of your disbelief and learn to trust what you receive. The only people I ever have seen who cannot communicate with animals are those who simply cannot let go of the idea that it's not supposed to be possible. If you have a block like that, it will be very difficult, if not impossible, to overcome it.

If you learn nothing else from this book, learn to trust that what you receive is real. You may receive words in your own voice or perhaps in a different voice. You may receive impressions, feelings, sensations, sights, sounds, and smells. The point is that you need to remain open to whatever comes through and believe it, without editing or judging.

Pawprint

Remain open to different forms of communication, and believe that what you receive is real.

Beginners often find it easier to communicate with animals other than their own pets. For some reason, we doubt information we receive from our own animal friends—we may think we "know" what they'd say or not want to believe what we think we're hearing. And sometimes, just as your children may tell a friend something they'd never tell you, your dog may prefer to talk to someone else (who may be less likely to reprimand him or to schedule a trip to the vet). Even after years of practice, I still confer with another communicator for validation if I feel some sort of lack in my conversations with my own pets.

You certainly can learn to communicate with animals on your own—if I did, then you can!—as long as you suspend your doubts at the beginning and simply trust that what you receive is real. But I also recommend learning animal communication either with partners or in a workshop atmosphere. Working with others (especially people you don't know) is a wonderful way to prove to yourself that you really can communicate telepathically. There's nothing like instant validation to take away your doubts!

Mark This Spot!

If you are interested in attending an animal communication workshop, check out my Web site at **www.goodpackleader.com** for more information, or e-mail me at **info@goodpackleader.com**.

EXERCISE 4

Sending and Receiving

There are some simple exercises that you can do that will introduce you to sending and receiving information and help you gain confidence in your ability. I've included some to do with a partner and some to do on your own.

WORKING WITH A PARTNER

Begin by sending a few easy messages in the form of visual images—color, shape, and a combination of the two. You can think up your own visual images as you do the exercise, or you can make up about a dozen index cards with a few simple shapes in different colors, one on each card. Use color/shape combinations other than those that are easily guessed, such as red hearts, green shamrocks, etc.; otherwise, you may find yourself guessing rather than receiving.

SEEING COLORS

Ready to try it? Here's what to do:

Sender: Pick an image or a card, and focus for several seconds on the item's color. Close your eyes, concentrate on the color, and then see it forming in your partner's mind.

Receiver: Close your eyes, focus on your "third eye" spot, and gently let yourself feel that you are receiving a color from your partner. When you recognize it, say it out loud.

Take turns sending and receiving. Don't be surprised if you "get it" on the first try. However, don't be discouraged if it takes a few tries. Just keep practicing until you feel comfortable with the process.

SEEING SHAPES

Now move on to the next step:

Sender: Pick an image or a card, and focus for several seconds on the item's shape. Close your eyes, concentrate on the shape, and then see it forming in your partner's mind.

Receiver: Repeat the steps for receiving mentioned above, letting yourself feel that you are receiving a shape from your partner. When you recognize it, say it out loud. Take turns sending and receiving.

SEEING COLORS AND SHAPES

Now let's put the two together:

Sender: Pick an image or a card, and focus for several seconds on the item's shape and color. Close your eyes, concentrate on the shape and its color, and then see it forming in your partner's mind.

Receiver: Repeat the steps for receiving mentioned above, letting yourself feel that you are receiving a colored shape from your partner. When you recognize it, say it out loud. Take turns sending and receiving.

WORKING ON YOUR OWN

To do these exercises by yourself, make the index cards as described and put them face down on a table. Choose one, hold it, and concentrate on it, all with your eyes closed. Feel the color, or shape, or combination coming into your head. When you feel recognition, look at the card to see how you've done. Alternatively, you could write down your answers and check them at the end. (Remember to keep the cards in the same order.)

EXERCISE 5

Talking to Dogs

Here's the exciting part—you're finally about to start talking to a dog! Once again, I'll tell you how to do this with a partner and then how to do it on your own. Relax, have fun, and enjoy your discoveries. You can do it!

WORKING WITH A PARTNER

When you and your partner feel comfortable sending and receiving basic shape and color information, you can attempt to send and receive information about each other's dogs, using photographs of the pets. This is an especially good technique to use with dogs who are unfamiliar to you. Here's how to do it:

1. To begin, you'll need clear photographs of each dog, showing the face, and a pen and paper. Pick about five simple, easily verifiable questions that you will each ask, and write them down ahead of time, leaving space for answers. Some suggestions include: What's your favorite toy? Where do you like to sleep? What treat do you like? Keep these questions very simple—now is not the time to get into potentially emotional issues (such as, Who do you like best? What do you think of the new baby?, etc.).

2. Exchange photographs. Then Partner 1 should write down basic information about Partner 2's dog: name, age, gender, and breed, if it's not obvious.

3. Partner 1: Hold the photograph of your partner's dog in front of you and concentrate on the dog's face. Silently say the dog's name, and feel your mind and heart opening. Take a moment and feel your spirit reaching out to the dog. Ask if she or he will speak with you, and listen for a reply. On occasion, you will receive a negative response; in that case, respect the dog's wishes, and try again later. If you don't get a definite "no," assume that the dog is willing.

4. When you feel that the dog has said "yes," begin to ask the questions silently, and *wait for an answer:* Are you happy? How do you feel? And so on. Take your time with each question, and write down any responses you receive. Remember, you actually may hear

a voice in your head, or you may receive feelings or impressions that you will have to interpret. Believe that whatever comes to you is real, and write it down without judging it.

5. When you have completed the five questions, ask the dog if she or he has anything more to say to you, and wait for a reply. When the conversation is finished, thank the dog, and say good-bye.

6. Share your answers with your partner. You may be surprised at how accurate the information is.

7. When you've finished discussing the conversation, begin again with Partner 2 speaking with Partner 1's dog.

One word of caution: If you talk with a dog who lives in a multianimal household, one of the other animals may "butt in" to the conversation. Don't worry about it now; simply write down whatever information you receive, and relay it to your partner. He or she may recognize some information as more relevant to a pet other than the one in the photograph.

WORKING ON YOUR OWN

To do this exercise by yourself, you can work with a photograph of your own dog, or you may want to borrow a photograph of a friend's dog (or two or three friends' dogs). Write down a few simple questions you plan to ask, put down the basic information (i.e., name, age, gender, and breed, if it's not your own dog), and then continue the exercise as described.

If you work with your own dog, *believe that what you receive is real, even if it doesn't sound "right" at first.* If you work with someone else's dog, you may want to share the information you received at a later time. This will give you the opportunity of outside validation.

PRACTICE

The most important thing to do now is practice, practice, practice! Telepathy is like any other skill—the more you do it, the better you become. Talk to your dog, your friends' dogs, dogs at the park, dogs anywhere. Remember that this technique also works with other animals and creatures; don't be afraid to try it with them as well.

In the next chapter, we'll look at how you can use your skills to interpret your dog's thoughts and influence his or her behavior.

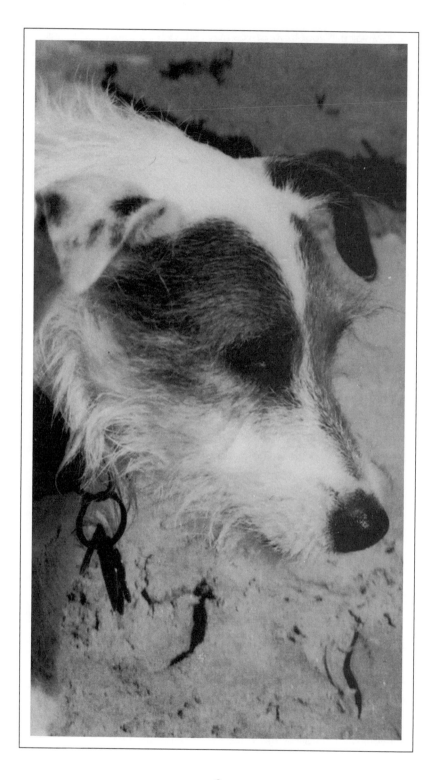

You and Your Dog

"The relationship between dogs and people has worked so well in part because both species are group-oriented—we both prefer to live with others—and in general, dogs are more inclined to be followers than leaders."

—Danika

Dogs have wormed their way into our hearts and families precisely because they have learned our language and behaviors so well and are eager to please. For many of us, they embody a host of fine human qualities, including loyalty, bravery, trust, and forgiveness, as well as others that are harder to find in humans, such as unconditional love, endless exuberance, and the ability to live in and enjoy the present moment.

COMMUNICATION: THEIRS AND OURS

A dog's innate ability to understand us goes further than most people think it does, and it takes a slightly different direction than you might expect. A dog's innate method of communicating with other members of his pack is largely nonverbal and involves postures, scents, facial expressions, and ritualistic behaviors. A pack leader does not need to voice a command; rather, his dominant behavior indicates to the pack who is in charge. Likewise, our dogs constantly interpret our body language in a way that makes sense to them. Although they are "bilingual," their own language—which is nonverbal—often is what they understand first.

Keep that in mind when you tell your pup verbally how much you dislike something he's done while thinking, "Awhhh, he's really cute when he does that." You might complete your reprimand by turning your face away, and in doing so, you betray your thoughts and signal submission. Not only do such mixed messages confuse the pup, but he most likely will take what he likes and disregard the rest...wouldn't you?

Therefore, begin to be aware of how your words, thoughts, and actions align with your intent. As far as possible, try keep them flowing in the same direction. For instance, imagine that your dog is beginning to run away from you. What do you do? Most of us shout, "Come here!" while thinking, "I just *know* he's going to keep running!" or picturing his furry behind receding in the distance. And what invariably happens? The dog obeys the thought or mind picture, right?

The next time this situation occurs, try a different approach. First, remain calm. Call your dog to come as you normally would, calmly and pleasantly, and at the same time visualize him coming to you and sitting at your feet. *Know* that he will respond, and expect him to. You may be pleasantly surprised at how well he hears that!

How Dogs Think

If you really want to understand your dog, learn a bit about the psychology of dogs and dog behavior. An excellent resource for such information is dog-behavior expert Cesar Millan of the Dog Psychology Center in Los Angeles. Millan has a unique understanding of dog psychology that he gained from his childhood experiences in Mexico, living on a farm around packs of dogs. His father and grandfather were canine *curanderos* (healers), and he himself feels an almost spiritual bond with dogs.

Millan now lives with a pack of about forty rehabilitated "pirate dogs" (i.e., dogs who were going to be euthanized because they were "vicious"). He is able to take these dogs on runs without leashes and feed them one at a time, in the midst of the pack, with no fights—precisely because he understands what it means to be a good pack leader.

Most dog trainers teach owners how to have their pets fulfill the needs of the human first, but Millan teaches people how to fulfill the dog's needs first. When the human does so, the dog then will happily and willingly fulfill the needs of the human, who becomes the pack leader. Creating such a dynamic involves connecting with the mind of the dog and then allowing that connection to follow through to the physical behaviors. Millan says that this new perspective involves training humans to understand their dogs as pack animals and rehabilitating the dogs so they return to their normal behavior as calm, submissive pack members.

Mark This Spot!

Check out Cesar Millan's TV show *The Dog Whisperer* and his Web site, **www.dogpsychologycenter.com**, for some amazing insights on being a good pack leader. Millan holds workshops for dog owners and also has produced a video of his techniques. Information about both is available at the Web site.

Remember that even though your dog is an individual and has his own personality traits, the majority of dogs prefer to be followers— they want a strong leader and are much happier if they know what's expected of them, rather than having to make all the decisions for themselves. In fact, when forced to take over the role of pack leader (which owners often unconsciously cause them to do), many dogs become anxious, jumpy, neurotic, and even aggressive, because the strain of leadership is too much for them. We should not forget as we stumble over ourselves to make them happy that all they want is to make us happy.

Inside Your Dog's Mind

Having some understanding of the canine psyche can help you understand your dog's behavior and may give you a new perspective on your communications with him or her. For instance, sometimes when you ask a question, the response might make no sense to you, but from the dog's point of view as a pack animal, it makes perfect sense. If you ask your dog why he barks incessantly whenever you leave the house without him, and he responds, "I can't see you," you may at first think he's just crazy about you (or just crazy). If you realize, however, that canines are most comfortable when they can see and be near other pack members and that they feel exposed and vulnerable when they're on their own, his response makes much more sense.

If a dog has assumed the role of pack leader, the "I can't see you" response may express something different: separation anxiety caused by the inability to keep control of all the pack members. Combining your knowledge of dog psychology with telepathic communication and the proper training techniques, you can develop a satisfactory solution for both you and your dog, such as letting him know how long you'll be gone, frequently "checking in" telepathically while you're away, and, of course, taking him for a nice long walk when you get home.

Once you understand what being a good pack leader means, you'll know better what your dog expects of you and how to make life happier for both of you.

CANINE CHILDREN

Many people say that they treat their dogs as if they were children, but they do not treat them as they would actually treat their own—and it's almost always detrimental to the dog. They really are saying that they allow their dogs to do anything they want, with few boundaries or limitations. Doing so creates spoiled, neurotic dogs who eventually become anxious, demanding, difficult to handle, and, unfortunately, too aggressive, which too often leads to the dog being removed from the family or even euthanized. It's a sad situation, made sadder still by the fact that it doesn't have to occur in the first place. It all could be avoided if dog owners simply understood more about the canine psychological makeup and how it differs from that of humans.

In some ways, dogs are very much like our children: They require guidance in addition to love. Being a good parent or a strong pack leader does not imply being "mean" or aggressive. Neither one is abusive; on the contrary, each is very loving. Both proclaim, "I'm here to guide you and ensure your safety and happiness. Rely on my direction to protect you." For both children and dogs, such guidance is a great relief, and it provides a sense of security that enables them to be themselves. The big difference between children and dogs is that most children will outgrow their need for constant guidance, and our canine friends will not.

Also like our children, dogs need a lot of exercise and mental stimulation. When the dog was first domesticated, it was a part of the family "pack" and had specific jobs to do, such as pulling a travois, finding prey, guarding flocks, or protecting children. In the modern, Western world, however, dogs have become more like trophies, often brought into the household as one more "prized possession," and may be left to wait hours for a few minutes of attention once or twice a day. Owners then become upset when they come home to shredded sofas, hole-filled yards, or peed-on beds, and they wonder why their dog drags them down the street like a sled when they finally go for a walk. Think about it. If you left your five-year-old alone in a house for eight or nine hours a day, what do you think you'd come home to? Worse yet, if you kept him locked in a small box such as a crate, with no stimulation whatsoever, how neurotic do you think he'd be?

On the one hand we lavish love and affection on our dogs and claim that they're valued members of the family, but on the other hand we treat them in a way that would be illegal if we did it to our children. It's no wonder that the majority of the consultations I do involve behaviors and emotional problems brought about by the difference between the human's lifestyle and expectations and the dog's interpretation of the situation.

Doggie Diaries

Tyler is an eight-month-old pit bull with whom I conversed over several months. Tyler is a friendly, sweet-hearted pup, but he had a nervous skin condition and the beginnings of dominant, neurotic behavior. His owner is a dog trainer who didn't seem to realize that Tyler needed the same guidance she gave her clients' dogs. She thought he was different because he was her "baby."

Because she couldn't take him with her to work, Tyler was crated for four or five hours a day because he wasn't yet housetrained, which left his owner feeling guilty. Often, he wasn't able to contain himself and soiled his crate, which resulted in a scolding as soon as his owner came home. Of course, Tyler had no idea why he was being scolded: he'd had no choice, and the soiling often had happened hours before, so he didn't understand that the scolding related to it. All he knew was that he was excited to see "Mom" and looked forward to some exercise and playtime. When he received a scolding first thing instead, he ended up thinking that he was not wanted.

Other emotional situations in the household added to this belief, and his resulting low self-esteem manifested in the skin condition and nervous, attention-getting behaviors, such as constantly jumping up, stealing and chewing personal belongings, and, eventually, nipping. Because of his owner's guilt over leaving him all day, she avoided correcting the bad behavior and instead lavished Tyler with affection in order to get him to stop. This treatment, of course, only reinforced the problematic behaviors: Regardless of whether Tyler was "bad" or "good," he got the attention he craved, but he still wasn't happy.

In addition, because he was a young, active pup, his boredom and frustration from being cooped up all day came out as destructive behavior, such as eating the couch and peeing on the bed whenever he was given free access to the house. Going for a walk involved lots of yanking and pulling as he dragged his owner down the street.

Fortunately, Tyler's owner loves him very much and was willing to change her own habits to help him get better. Tyler needed a pack leader to guide him lovingly in how to behave and to give clear instructions about what was expected of him. He needed a lot more exercise coupled with discipline, and he needed a job to do to keep his mind stimulated. He also needed reassurance that, regardless of the emotional situations involving other members of the family, he was loved and wanted.

Over the course of several months and numerous consultations, we worked together to bring peace to this household. When I asked Tyler what he wanted to do for exercise, he relayed that he wanted to do "the running and jumping thing" (dog agility courses), which he had seen at demonstrations with his owner. I also suggested that his owner think of Tyler as a small child in need of a good parent who would provide boundaries and limitations through consistent discipline. As a dog trainer, she already knew how to do this; she just needed to see that good discipline is not being "mean," and that Tyler would be much happier once he knew exactly what was expected of him.

To help with the exercising, she bought a small cart for Tyler to pull when they walked. Because pit bulls easily can pull more than thirty times their body weight, Tyler is well suited for helping to carry groceries, haul gardening supplies, or even relocate the pile of rocks in the backyard. These jobs helped Tyler feel important and also tired him out, so that waiting for "Mom" to come home was an opportunity for sleep instead of for destructive play.

I'm happy to say that as his owner reassessed her own behavior and understood what Tyler really needed and wanted, Tyler's skin condition started to disappear, he stopped soiling his crate, and he continues to learn how to be a good pack member. This example shows how a combination of animal communication, an understanding of dog psychology, and good training habits can work together as an integrated therapy.

— From Danika's Casebook

Mark This Spot!

There are many good books and videos on dog training, as well as classes that you and your dog can take. Do a little research, and look for nonviolent methods of training that provide positive reinforcement and respect the dog's needs as well as your own. A good place to start is with the helpful resources at the back of this book (beginning on page 198), as well as on my Web site (**www.goodpackleader.com**).

THE IMPORTANCE OF EXERCISE

A big yard does not relieve you of the responsibility to exercise your dog—a yard is just a bigger box than the house, no matter how many toys are in it. Therefore, if you don't have the time to walk your dog every day, you don't have time to have a dog. Period. If you have a schedule that requires you to be away regularly for many hours or even days at a time, consider hiring someone to walk your dog during your absence. Please think long and hard before you get a dog and always be sure to select a breed with traits that fit your lifestyle not just one whose appearance appeals to you. We'll talk more about choosing a dog in the next chapter.

Mark This Spot!

Jodi Andersen's book *The Latchkey Dog* gives an in-depth look at "how the way you live shapes the behavior of the dog you love," which also is the subtitle of the book. If your dog is at home alone during the day, this book is an indispensable resource.

Exercise is a great tension reliever for your dog, just as it is for you. When dogs spend a lot of time waiting for their owners, they build up tension and stress that, if not vented through proper exercise, may boil over into behavior problems such as obsessive barking, digging, chewing, and other annoying, destructive habits like Tyler's. Dogs with active natures especially will benefit from a long walk, and they may need even more stimulation and exercise than that. Try asking your dog what she'd like to do.

I spoke once with Nalla, a Lab/Australian blue heeler mix, whose owner was stressed out about a job he hated and agonizing over whether to move to Colorado and be a ski instructor. His indecision was caused partly by his concern over how Nalla would handle the move and the colder climate. Her response was, "I'd love to be trained as a ski rescue dog. I love the snow, I love being with him, and my previous owners used to take me with them when they went skiing. Please tell him 'let's go!'"

Another option for active dogs is to try something directly related to their breed. For example, if you have a retired greyhound, try contacting other greyhound owners to organize a weekly "race" at the dog park. If you have a Bouvier de Flanders or Border collie, check into taking him to herding school. Even getting a backpack for your dog and having him carry the water bottles on a long hike can provide extra exercise and will help him feel useful. Chapter 8 offers many ideas on places to go and things to do with your dog.

Remember that many behavior issues can be avoided easily by exercising your dog to a pleasantly worn-out state on a regular basis. If he's tired, he won't want to start digging up your yard or chewing up your furniture!

In addition to providing him with exercise, walking with your dog is an excellent way to increase your emotional bond with each other. You can easily combine exercise and discipline during a walk by using it as an opportunity to reinforce your position as beloved pack leader. Your dog will love you for it.

Mark This Spot!

If your large dog regularly takes you for a drag, consider using a lead that controls the head, such as a Halti or Gentle Leader®. These leads are *not* muzzles, although they have a strap that gently encircles the dog's nose. When properly fitted, these halter-type leads use the dog's natural pressure points and opposition reflex to provide calm, humane control within minutes, while retaining the dog's ability to breathe, eat, and drink comfortably. They are better for many people to use than choke chains or collars, which often are misplaced at the base of the neck where they trigger the dog's natural instinct to pull and, if used improperly, can seriously damage the dog's trachea and spine.

Pawprint

If you plan to use a choke chain or collar, learn to use it correctly! It is *not* used for punishment but rather to grab the dog's attention. Timing is critical: You must use a short snap-*and-release* motion—*not* a pull-until-the-dog-chokes gesture. Placement also is critical: The collar should be placed high on the neck, above the Adam's apple, and right behind the ears, *never* down low across the trachea and base of the neck—watch a dog show to see how professionals do it. And *never* leave a choke chain on your dog when you're not training him or her; it's too easy for the dog to be strangled with it. Leads such as the Halti and Gentle Leader (see above) let you control your dog without the potential hazards of a choke chain.

Doggie Diaries

While doing some extended housesitting for friends, I had the wonderful opportunity to work with Josh, a 7-year-old, nearly 100-pound Siberian husky, and Aliya, a two-year-old, roughly 50-pound Samoyed. They are beautiful, sweet-hearted dogs who are bred to work and happy to please. But by the end of a 20-minute walk, I knew exactly what it feels like to be a dogsled! Because I have back and neck problems, I was not really able to walk both dogs at once, and even walking one at a time left me aching and sore.

After a little investigation, I asked my friends if I could use a Gentle Leader® on Josh, and they agreed. This type of halter-lead activates the calming pressure point on the neck behind the ears (the same spot a mother dog grasps to pick up a puppy) and also mimics the gentle "nose grab" a pack leader will use to assert control.

After communicating to Josh that I wanted to try something new and that I would like his cooperation, I followed the directions to fit him properly. At first, Josh found the lead to be somewhat uncomfortable, but it was more the newness than anything else. As we started, I asked him to continue to cooperate, and I told him that I was going to be the leader for this walk. As I said, Josh has a sweet personality, and although he's been used to getting his way, he decided to play along.

He expressed his annoyance at the nose piece a couple of times, but once we both got the hang of the new lead, he hardly noticed it at all. We were walking at the same speed as before, but within five or ten minutes, Josh fell into place beside me, rarely pulling ahead at all. I was happy, and I let him know how much I appreciated his cooperation.

When I used this combination of techniques—communication, tools, and attitude—walking with Josh became a completely different experience. There were a few instances when reminders were necessary, but that is to be expected whenever you try to change a longstanding behavior. As a result of this experience, I now look forward to my opportunities to take Josh for a walk, and we can go for a longer period of time simply because

I'm not worn out within the first ten minutes. He's happier, and I'm happier. Aliya also has done well with her regular cloth choke collar placed high on her neck—no more pulling and coughing the entire walk—and now I can walk Josh and her at the same time.

— From Danika's Casebook

Now that you know more about how dogs see the world—and what they expect from you as their fearless leader—you're ready to turn to the next chapter and find out how to choose the best dog for you. If you already have a dog, read along. And if you decide to expand your canine family—what you'll learn in Chapter 4 will really come in handy!

Using Intuition to Choose the Right Dog

*"One day I was delivering my usual donation of
a bag of food to the local shelter. It was a few
minutes before opening time, and I was waiting
outside, near a pen where some dogs were enjoying
the sunshine. All of a sudden, one of them came
up to the fence and looked me straight in the eye,
and I had this eerie feeling that it was my beloved
terrier, who had passed away several years earlier.
'Socrates? Is that you?' I blurted. The scruffy
mixed-breed mutt looked at me steadily, made
that funny sneezing sound Socrates always made,
and I knew it was my old pal come back to me.
As soon as the doors opened, I went straight to
the desk and arranged to adopt him!"*

—Kendra T.

Since the days of the first domesticated dogs, humans have recognized the unusual bond that our two species share. A dog, just by its presence, adds so much to a household. It's no wonder that there are 65 million pet dogs in the United States—and almost a quarter of those live with one or more canine companions.

Animal communication can help you select the right dog to share your life with. Note, however, that it is only one of the tools you'll need to use to make such an important choice. Before you rush out to find your own furry ball of love, there are a few things you should do.

First Things First

First, and most importantly, educate yourself about dog ownership. In many ways, getting a dog is similar to becoming a parent: There are many of the same responsibilities, especially with a puppy, and it is a major decision that requires a lot of soul-searching and preparation. It should not be taken lightly. Remember that although children eventually grow up and take on their own responsibilities, a dog will need to be walked, groomed, fed, taken to the vet, cleaned up after, and so on throughout his or her life.

Humane shelters and rescue organizations are overflowing with pets who were purchased on a whim, with no forethought, planning, or education about the realities of caring for them. Don't be one of those careless individuals who treat animals so callously—we're talking about a living being here not a car! Now that you've learned to communicate with dogs, you know they have feelings and attachments just as people do, and you must respect that fact.

One more request: Please don't be one of those misguided individuals who gets a dog and then keeps it tied in the yard or fenced in a kennel far from the house. Such an existence would be sad and lonely for any creature, but it is even worse for a dog, who is a social animal and needs interaction with other pack members (i.e., your family) to be secure and happy.

SOME IMPORTANT QUESTIONS TO ASK

Make sure you know your own feelings—and your family's—about important issues of dog ownership before you take the plunge. Ask yourself the following questions:

1. Why do I want a dog?

2. How will a dog fit in with my lifestyle?

3. How much time do I have to spend with a dog?

4. Do I have the money to afford vet bills, grooming, food, leashes, toys, beds, treats, boarding kennels or pet sitters, etc.?

5. Do I want an active dog who needs lots of exercise or one that likes to lay around a lot?

6. Are my kids ready to share the house with a dog? Will they be willing and able to participate in the dog's care?

7. Am I willing to commit to the loving care of another being for potentially fifteen to twenty years, in sickness and in health,

for richer and for poorer, changing my schedule to accommodate my dog, walking in all kinds of weather, getting dog hair on everything I own, and dealing with occasional diarrhea, vomiting, or worse? In other words, am I willing to make a commitment for a *lifetime, no matter what?*

These questions are not meant to scare you but rather to give you an honest picture of what to expect. As I said earlier, in my opinion, the decision to get a dog is as important as the decision to have a child. You must answer these questions honestly.

Getting a dog to relieve loneliness, provide companionship, or fulfill an emotional need is fine, as long as you remember that the dog has his own emotional, physical, and mental needs as well—and that those needs are different than a human's. This relationship should be *mutually gratifying*—the care you give will be rewarded a thousand times over.

Mark This Spot!

Lucky for us dog owners and wannabe dog owners, there are some excellent resources available to help us. Check out the award-winning Web site **http://loveyourdog.com** to help kids learn about dog ownership (note that lack of "www" in the URL). Pedigree pet food company's educational site at **www.pedigree.com** has information about responsible dog ownership, breed info, and more.

There's also a nationwide public service called Pets 911 to help people across the country quickly and easily find the local pet-related information they need. Pets 911 consists of a Web site (**www.Pets911.com**) and a toll-free, automated hotline (1-888-PETS-911) that allows pet lovers to access local information about adoptable pets, emergency veterinary hospitals, pet-friendly apartments, and much more. Best of all, it's free!

Doggie Diaries

You can get a taste of dog ownership by offering to take care of a friend's dog for the weekend or while he or she is on vacation. Doing so is an excellent way to "try out" doggie duties and to spend some extended time in the company of a canine companion. If you have several friends with different breeds of dogs, you have a wonderful opportunity to get first-hand experience with different temperaments and personalities and to practice your animal communication. That is exactly how I developed wonderful friendships with Josh and Aliya, a Siberian husky and Samoyed pair; with Luke, a Lab/golden retriever mix; and with Nikki, a shih tzu.

How Much Does That Doggie Cost?

Don't let yourself be fooled: The purchase price or adoption fee is only the beginning of what it costs to have a dog in the family. Learn about the expenses involved in owning a dog—your friends are a good source of this information. Ask them how much shots and vet visits cost and which vets they recommend. Ask what they pay for grooming, pet sitters, trainers, and doggie daycare.

Find out what's available in your area and what it costs. Research how much various breeds eat in a month and how much that will cost. Visit a pet store and check out the prices for leashes, collars, toys, treats, beds, and the other accessories that are part and parcel of the wonderful world of dog ownership.

Picking a Breed

Thanks to our human need for change, there are hundreds of dog breeds, ranging from the ultra-small "teacup" varieties that could fit in your pocket to the extra-large types that could fill a small room.

Pawprint

CAUTION: Some insurance companies have started charging steep premiums or even canceling the homeowner policies of clients who prefer large, powerful breeds such as rottweilers, German shepherds, Doberman pinschers, Akitas, pit bulls, or chows. Although insurers claim that the change is due to an increase in liability claims stemming from dog bites, the practice forces owners to choose between their insurance policy and their dog. Unfortunately, it results in many pets being relinquished to shelters and rescue organizations. Therefore, check with your insurance company *before* you decide on a breed. If your heart's set on one of the penalized breeds, check out **www.hsus.org** to see what you can do to fight the bans.

In addition to the purebreds, there are millions of dogs of mixed parentage that embody the best of several breeds to make superb all-around pets.

Some will argue that certain breeds are more susceptible to certain illnesses and diseases as a result of their breeding and that mixed breeds (or "mongrels") tend to be healthier. Others say that responsible breeding weeds out the traits that cause greater susceptibility to illness. Your best bet is to educate yourself about the pros and cons and then decide what works best for you.

Take some time to search the Internet and your local library for information about different breeds. There are thousands of Web sites and books devoted to dogs and dog ownership, and every breed has fans who are more than happy to provide you with lots of helpful information. Look for a Pet Expo coming to your area—it will bring breeders, rescue organizations, suppliers, and service providers all together in one convenient location. You'll also need to know about grooming requirements, temperament, and characteristics to see which breed is a good match for your family and lifestyle, and all of these resources, as well as those listed in the back of this book, will help you find the answers you need.

It's also vital to know what kind of exercise a particular breed requires—some breeds, including terriers, dalmatians, and greyhounds, need lots of opportunities to run in addition to their regular walks. If you don't have a large yard, you'll have to find a safe area to accommodate this, such as a dog park. Other breeds, such as Newfoundlands and Great Danes, are not high-energy dogs, and they are happy to lay around between walks. Dogs like pit bulls, rottweilers, Bouviers, Border collies, shepherds, and other herding or working breeds need mental stimulation as well as lots of exercise—a short walk is apt to leave them frustrated and bored, which translates into yards full of holes and furniture torn to shreds. Even small dogs like Chihuahuas, toy poodles, and Shih tzus require regular exercise; lap dogs who never leave the lap get fat and grumpy.

Mark This Spot!

As mentioned above, check out the Internet for Pet Expos coming to your area. They're lots of fun, and they'll provide you with tons of free information about different breeds and offer the latest in pet supplies. Also try Web sites such as **www.pedigree.com** and **www.ivillage/pets/dogs** for breed specifics, including susceptibility to illness.

RESCUE ORGANIZATIONS, BREEDERS, AND SHELTERS

Once you start looking for a dog, where should you go? The four most popular options are rescue organizations, breeders, shelters, and classified ads. Let's look at the pros and cons of each.

Rescue Organizations

When you're trying to decide on a breed, be sure to check out the rescue organizations. They're invariably run by incredible people who have a special place in their hearts for a particular breed of dog. These groups are often the best source for honest, reliable information about their favorite breed, because they've seen too many dogs abandoned, abused, or given up because of someone's poor preparation for dog ownership.

If you choose to adopt a rescue dog, expect to be given a thorough interview, a house visit or two, and possibly even specific requirements prior to adoption—these dedicated people are searching for the right "forever home" for their dogs, and they would rather turn down an applicant than risk further traumatizing a dog by having it returned to them.

Adopting a rescued dog used to be much riskier than it is now. Today's reputable rescue organizations are very thorough in their efforts to determine the cause of a dog's surrender to them, and they are extremely careful when matching a dog with a new family. Many groups have trained foster families that work specifically with abused animals, helping them to regain their trust in humans and their ability to live with a family. This interval can last for months if a dog has been severely traumatized.

Mark This Spot!

A great place to start in your search for a dog to adopt is www.petfinder.com, a Web site that helps you adopt a homeless pet. It has links to thousands of rescue organizations and shelters across the country, as well as listings of hundreds of thousands of pets that need homes, many with photos. The Web site also has a large library of information on different breeds and about pet ownership.

Some organizations now train their volunteers and foster families in animal communication, which is a fantastic way to help them do their job. It gives voice to the dog's concerns, provides insights into their past situations and possible solutions, and sometimes can help find unseen medical conditions that may have caused bad behavior.

If you have your heart set on a particular breed of dog, please seriously consider working with a rescue organization. Not only will you be saving a life, but often the members of the group turn out to be lifelong friends!

Breeders

If you choose to work with a breeder, please, please, *please* be sure that you find a reputable one. The last thing this planet needs is more unwanted puppies brought into the world by some "backyard breeder" who thinks it would be great to make $500 on each of his or her dog's precious offspring. Dogs are not moneymaking machines!

Reputable breeders know and care about every dog they produce. They know the characteristics of both parents and their respective lineages, keep scrupulous records, and welcome your questions. In fact, they probably will require a good deal of information about you and your family to ensure that each pup is going to a good home. The best breeders take lifetime responsibility for every one of their dogs and require you to return your dog to them if for any reason you must give it up.

Check a particular breed's official Web site for a list of local breeders sanctioned by the national dog associations. Ask friends and family for recommendations as well. Then visit, ask questions, and get a feel for the breeders and their dogs. If anything at all causes you to feel wary, go to another breeder.

Note that good breeders put a lot into their breeding programs, work with fine bloodlines, and provide excellent facilities, training, and healthcare. All of that is reflected in the puppy's price, so a dog from a good breeder won't be cheap! If you want a purebred puppy, be prepared to invest in him or her.

Humane Societies

Selecting a dog from a humane society is another way to save a life. Now that you have been honing your animal communication skills, this option will be less risky as well. The price is right, too—usually adoption fees at shelters are very modest.

Many fine pups have ended up at a shelter for no other reason than their owners tired of them, moved and couldn't take them along, or got a new job that took them on the road all the time. Indeed, only a small percentage of the dogs at shelters are strays.

Check your local phone book for the nearest SPCA or Humane Society. You also can use the Petfinder Web site or the Pets 911 service mentioned previously (**www.petfinder.com, www.Pets911.com** and **1-888-PETS-911**). These sites help people around the country access information about local pets for adoption. You can scan through pictures of homeless pets posted by several hundred animal shelters and adoption groups, and you can search by breed and other characteristics. The extensive, informative Web site of the Humane Society of the United States (**www.hsus.org**) also offers listings and help. You just may find your next best friend online!

Classified Ads

You may see an ad in the paper or a note on a bulletin board that tugs at your heartstrings. My advice is to have a long conversation with the dog's present owners and make sure you're actually considering buying (or adopting) someone's pet—not getting a pup from a backyard breeder or puppy mill (see "What *Not* to Do" on page 73). People give up their dogs for many reasons—they have to move, a child is allergic to him, the dog is loud or destructive, it's too much responsibility, they're too busy, they have too many pets—you name it. Try to find out why the family is listing their pet before you go out to see him or her. Obviously, it's much easier to integrate a well-behaved dog into your home life and routines than it is to integrate one who, usually because of poor handling by the original owner, barks constantly, chews the furniture, or is aggressive.

When you answer a private ad, you may be rescuing a perfectly wonderful dog before it's dumped at a shelter or rescue organization. But the same rule applies here as to any other case in which you're considering a new pet: If you go to meet him and you don't feel that he's the "one," don't let yourself be guilt-tripped into taking him. Thank the people, and continue your search.

Usually, if the ad is for someone's pet, it will be "free to a good home" or reasonably priced, although if someone has bought an expensive purebred, they may try to recoup at least part of the purchase price. Bear in mind that as far as cost goes, paying for someone else's problems will be very expensive in the long run, even if the dog is free—and a good dog is priceless, however much or little it costs.

What Not to Do

Please stay away from pet stores and puppy mills. Most often, "that doggy in the window" has come from a puppy mill and is a behavioral and medical disaster on four legs. Puppy mills are horrid places where dogs are treated as commodities. Because the animals are bred indiscriminately, diseases and genetic problems often run rampant. And because medical care and love are mostly nonexistent, the dogs and puppies are subject to untold suffering and most certainly are not treated as living beings who deserve respect.

Pawprint

STOP! Don't support puppy mills! Go to the Web site of the Humane Society of the United States at **www.hsus.org** and type "puppy mills" into the search box for extensive information about puppy mills and what you can do to help.

You may think that you're saving a life by getting a puppy from such a place, but in reality, you're simply contributing to the continued existence of puppy mills, and you may end up with a dog that has lifelong medical and emotional problems. Instead, I highly recommend joining a humane group that is working to shut down these disgusting displays of human greed and heartless cruelty.

Connecting to That Special Someone

Now that you've done your homework and made the decision that being part of a lifelong friendship with a canine companion is for you, begin the process of actually finding the right dog using your telepathic skills.

Remember the Sacred Clearing visualization I took you through in Chapter 2? Use it again now to start to "call" your new friend to you. (See page 37 for a refresher on how it's done.)

EXERCISE 6

Connecting to Your New Dog

If you have chosen a specific breed of dog with whom you'd like to share your home, it may help you to focus your attention on a picture of that breed. Note that you are not focusing on the dog in the picture but on the general qualities of the breed. If you feel that the right dog will come to you without such a specific request, then a photo is not necessary. You also may want to have a pen and paper handy so that you can record any pertinent details when the visualization is over.

Prepare yourself for this visualization by performing whatever simple ritual you have created for yourself. (See page 42 for more on creating an appropriate ritual.) You may wish to connect with your Spirit Guide (see page 39), and ask for his or her assistance. When you are ready, begin the Sacred Clearing visualization as before: Sit comfortably, breathe slowly, and follow the same path through the field, through the woods, and to the comfortable resting spot on the warm, ancient rocks.

Here's what to do next:

1. Relax with your eyes closed, listening to the breeze and the music of the crickets, frogs, birds, and bees all around you. Feel the warmth from the rocks beneath you and the sun above you.

2. As you rest there, begin to think about your dog. Silently ask your Spirit Guide to help you in your quest to find your new friend. If you seek a specific type of dog, focus on the details of the breed: the color, shape of the face, feel of the fur, etc. If you don't have a breed in mind, softly focus your thoughts on your dog, so you can look into his or her eyes.

3. Begin to shape a mental image of your dog, and silently call her or him to you with your heart. A name may come to you in the stillness; if it does, repeat it silently as you continue to focus your mind and heart on your dog. After a little while, you may feel a presence beside you. If you do, notice whatever details are clear. Don't be disappointed if everything is not clear; rest assured that your new friend has heard and at this very moment is beginning the journey to you.

4. You also may see or discern details of the surroundings where you will find your pet, such as the outside of a particular building, scenes through a window, furnishings in a room, or even other animals. Take note of them.

5. Tell your dog that you are ready to accept the commitment of a lifelong friendship and that you would like to meet him or her in the physical world. Ask if there are any clues or details that will help you know how to reach and identify him or her.

6. Let your focus return to your heart, and focus on making a connection from your heart to your new friend's heart. Some people like to visualize a silver thread or golden cord connecting the two. Whatever you use to visualize the connection, concentrate on gently making it stronger.

7. When you feel ready, thank your dog for visiting with you, and say how much you already love him or her. Let your new friend know how happy you'll be when you finally meet and that you will be

looking for him or her from now on. Then say good-bye until you meet again.

8. Return along the path through the woods, breathing deeply and noticing once again the sights, sounds, and smells of the forest. Go back through the open field, noticing the fragrances of the wildflowers and the sounds of the birds and other flying creatures. Feel the warmth of the sun on your skin.

9. Once you are back where you began, slowly return your awareness to your body. Mentally center and ground yourself by feeling the floor beneath your feet. Gently open your eyes. Record whatever information you received, without judging it, especially if it was not what you were expecting.

This reaching-out visualization will put the gears of the Universe in motion, for it will surely send whatever you call to you. However, the time frame is not guaranteed, and you will have to trust that your pup will appear at the right time—your job at this point is to remain alert for signals and to recognize the right time to act. Read about Jessie and Sam below to see what I mean.

Doggie Diaries

A few years ago, after I took an animal communication workshop, I started thinking about getting a dog. Every once in a while, I'd see someone's new puppy and think how wonderful it would be to have my own furry little bundle of energy. Before I actually began my search in earnest, however, a name would pop into my head whenever I thought about dogs: "Sam," as in Samantha. I thought it was odd at first, but it got clearer each time I'd look at a book about dogs, or visit a friend who had a dog, or just daydream about "my" dog.

I eventually decided to try to contact Sam, whoever she was, in meditation. Although it took a couple of tries, Sam finally decided to show herself to me—and she was a beautiful, honey-colored golden retriever pup, about three months old. I was ecstatic to put a face with the name at last! I was not able to get much information about how and where we would meet, but Sam assured me it would be within one month and that I would recognize her when I saw her. She was very clear about one thing: I was not to go looking for her. She would find me when she was ready.

Of course I was anxious about the whole thing, and I wondered what I could do to make it happen sooner rather than later, but I knew that I had to let things take their own course. About three weeks later, I stopped at a local convenience store for a cup of coffee, and there, on the bulletin board, was a flier with a color photo of a gorgeous honey-colored golden retriever puppy and the words, "Please Help! Sam needs a loving home! Toddler is allergic!" written underneath, with the phone number and a few other details. I couldn't believe my eyes! There was my Sam, grinning right at me from the photo, just waiting for me to call!

I didn't even wait to get home: I just grabbed the flier and went straight to the pay phone. My call was answered by a lovely woman who explained that the family had only had Sam for a few weeks, and that they all absolutely loved the puppy but that, unfortunately, their two-year-old son had a severe allergy to her. They hated giving her up, and they hoped to find someone in the area that would allow them to visit with her occasionally.

When I explained a little bit about my story, the woman was very excited and asked if I wanted to come over right away. I quickly agreed and drove to their house.

I wasn't even out of my car when Sam's little body appeared in the living room window, barking happily and wagging excitedly. After I was welcomed into the house, the woman told me she'd never seen Sam do anything like that before—she usually waited until a guest was actually inside to start her antics.

This is one story with a very happy ending: Sam and I went home together that day, and we have been constant companions ever since. We're training together to work in the local hospital's therapy dog program, and we see Sam's "other family" on regular occasions.

—Jessie L.

You may or may not receive messages as clearly as Jessie did—don't worry. Remain open to the possibility of finding the perfect dog for you, and it will happen. Once you have set the stage using the Sacred Clearing visualization for your pup to come to you, there are a few things you may want to try to "grease the rails," so to speak.

For example, if you have decided on a particular breed of dog, start by asking for recommendations from friends or veterinarians for reputable breeders or rescue associations. If you would be happy with whatever breed "chooses" you and would like to save a life in the process, you may want to start by visiting local animal shelters or scanning newspaper ads.

Pawprint

CAUTION! When checking newspaper ads, avoid promoting "backyard" breeding and puppy mills. Look for ads that clearly are placed by people looking for a good home for their pet. And don't be afraid to ask questions!

EXERCISE 7

Using the Pendulum

If you're like me, you like to get as much information as possible before making a big decision. Dowsing with a pendulum over a particular ad or a location on a map can offer some insights from your Inner Self, which already has all the answers. Using this technique is certainly not required, but you may find it helpful.

Using a pendulum is very easy—you can learn it in a few minutes. You may use a fancy crystal or stone pendulum (available from New Age shops and rock shops) if you wish, but all you really need is a piece of string and something with a little weight to hang from it, such as a small stone. You even can use a pendant necklace. Most dowsers prefer an item made from a natural substance, such as stone, metal, or wood, because they feel that it resonates with Earth energies better than man-made products do. The idea is that the pendulum must be heavy enough to swing on its own (so a paper clip won't work).

To use a pendulum, gently grasp the string or chain with your thumb and forefinger several inches above the pendulum object, allowing it to swing freely while your elbow rests comfortably on a flat surface.

This type of dowsing works well for providing answers to "yes or no" questions and for providing numerical values. First, however, you must determine what constitutes a "yes" answer and what constitutes a "no." Begin by sitting comfortably at a table. Holding the pendulum at the appropriate spot with your thumb and forefinger, and with your elbow resting on the table, gently arch your wrist so that the pendulum can swing freely in any direction without bumping your arm. Some people find that dowsing works better when they hold the pendulum with their nondominant hand. Try it both ways to see what works best for you.

Bring the pendulum to a complete stop with your other hand. Focus your attention on the pendulum, keep your arm and hand still, and silently ask, "Show me a 'yes.'" The pendulum may start to swing left to right, forward and back, or possibly in a circle—each person's answer may be different. Note the direction, and stop the pendulum's movement again. Then silently ask, "Show me a 'no.'" Once again, note the direction in which the pendulum begins to swing. You may want to write down the answers—I know it sounds silly, with only two possibilities, but you may later find yourself asking, "Now which way was 'no'?" and having to repeat the whole process.

Once you've determined the yes and no responses, begin asking questions using the newspaper ad or a map location (e.g., of a breeder or a person's home). With the pendulum poised over the ad, you might ask, "Is this where my dog is?" or "Is this the right dog for me?" and then watch for the answer. You can do the same thing with a map showing a breeder's location or even use the breeder's business card. You can ask the same questions or any others you choose.

First Contact

The next step is to prepare to meet your dog. Now's another great
time to use those psychic communication skills you've been building.
Whether you're answering an ad or responding to a listing from
a shelter, rescue organization, or breeder will help you determine
which technique to use. Let's go through them slowly so you can get
them down pat. Then, when the moment comes, you'll be ready!

Answering an Ad

If you call someone about an advertisement, get as much information
as you can about the situation. If you like what you hear and decide
to visit, schedule the visit with an allowance for some time to do a
telepathic communication. Then, using the same techniques you
learned in Chapter 2, attempt to communicate with the dog from the
ad. If you have a photo, great; if not, the information that you took
over the phone—description, gender, breed, age—is enough to work
with. Remember first to ask the dog if you may ask questions; don't
just start right in with a barrage of queries.

Keep your session fairly short and to the point, and remember to
ask the dog for any input he or she may have. You can ask whatever
you feel is important, but you'll probably want to know the reasons
for leaving the current family (the dog's version may be different
than the owners'), the state of the dog's physical and mental health,
whether the dog has any concerns about leaving or any special needs
or requests, etc. When you've completed the conversation, thank the
dog for cooperating, and if you feel clearly one way or another, let
the dog know. It's not fair to leave him or her wondering or hoping if
you've already made up your mind.

If your conversation leads you to believe that this dog is for
you, then, by all means, visit as soon as possible. You may find a
very ecstatic welcome waiting for you. Continue your conversation
with the dog when you visit—try to arrange for a few quiet moments
alone with him or her to confirm the information you received earlier.
If everything seems in order, you've found your new lifetime friend!

Visiting a Breeder, Shelter, or Rescue Organization

If you decide to visit a breeder, shelter, or rescue organization to look for your dog, prepare yourself before you leave home. Spend a few quiet minutes clearing your mind. If you wish, ask your Spirit Guide(s) to assist you. (See page 39 for more about finding your Spirit Guide.) Visualize a golden cord or silver thread reaching out from your heart to the heart of your dog, and let him or her know that you are on your way. Take a moment to listen for any feedback you may receive.

Once you arrive at the location, calmly take in the surroundings and meet the dogs. Note any feelings you have or any communication you receive from the animals. One animal may stand out from the rest. If possible, arrange for a few quiet moments with the dogs, and see if any particular one calls to you in some way. Ask questions like the ones I suggested above.

If the dog is a rescue, ask him for any information about his past that he may care to share. Such information is most helpful in identifying physical or mental traumas and what kind of help the dog may need. Be honest if the situation is more than you can handle. If you feel comfortable doing so, talk with someone at the rescue organization about the information you received if you think it will help them find the dog a home.

If you don't feel anything in particular (other than a happy feeling of being around a whole bunch of canines), it may be because your future pal isn't there. Don't try to force the issue. Come back another day, and try again.

If, on the other hand, you feel a clear signal that "the one" is there with you, visualize the golden cord and silently ask that your pup identify him- or herself. You may also ask your Guide to help you find the right one. When the connection is made, you will know it, I assure you. That recognition in the eyes is unmistakable. All that's left is the paperwork and the ride home, and then you'll begin one of the most satisfying journeys of your life!

Homeward Bound

Here's a suggestion for the homecoming: Be prepared to take your new friend for a long walk *before* taking him or her into your home. There are several reasons to do so. First, dogs that have been kept in kennels or cages for a period of time generally have not had a lot of exercise. Second, they've been subjected to a lot of commotion and stress; this and the ride in a strange new automobile may cause anxiety that a good long walk will relieve. Third, the walk is an excellent opportunity for you to introduce yourself as the new pack leader in a friendly way on neutral territory. And last, a walk allows both of you to transition from strangers to friends before having to share living space. You're going to be together for a lifetime, so you may as well start off on the right foot (and paw)!

What's Your Name?

Some people really get into the whole naming process, whether it's for a new dog or a new child. They enjoy searching baby naming books, Web sites, etc., trying to pick just the right one. However, as a person who communicates with animals, selecting a name for your new friend poses an interesting opportunity: You can find out from your dog what his or her name is or allow your dog to pick a suitable name. It's simple: Just ask, and then *listen*.

If you have a special affinity for a certain name, or would like to choose a name with a particular meaning, you certainly can offer suggestions. However, I think it's a wonderful idea to work with our pets to discover what moniker suits them, especially if you are adopting an older dog who may wish to keep or change his current name, depending on the situation he left behind. Ask your dog what name he would like to use and whether it is acceptable to use a nickname or "pet name" (no pun intended!).

When you are picking a name for a puppy, keep in mind that names do have meanings, so try to choose something that fits your dog's personality. Not every rottweiler is a "Brutus," and not every miniature poodle needs to be called "Fifi." And although some dogs may appreciate a tag like "Bonzo," others most certainly would be offended.

Using Your Dog's Name

Here is a very important point and a mistake that many pet owners make: Use your dog's name only for praise. A simple sound like "Sshh!" can be used consistently to correct a behavior. Never call your dog's name and then issue punishment when he responds, unless you want to train him to ignore you whenever you call him by his name. Let's face it: Would you come running to get yelled at?

One more thing: Please remember that using nasty epithets is unacceptable. Terms like "Stupid," "Knucklehead," "Bonehead," and the like should never be used when speaking to or about your dog. I am here to tell you that they understand *exactly* what you're saying, and that they will behave accordingly.

As an example, I once worked with a client who brought home a Sheltie puppy without prior discussion with or the consent of her husband. He was not fond of dogs, and he continually called the new puppy "that stupid dog." Within a couple of months, this poor animal was so convinced that the husband hated her and wanted to get rid of her that she developed a skin rash and a host of anxiety behaviors.

Luckily, when I told the woman that her dog was sick because of the verbal abuse and negative atmosphere in the house, she managed to convince her husband to change his mind and start over with the puppy. Now they're working toward a much happier environment for all of them.

You're off to a great start—you've found your dog, brought her home, and learned her name. In the next chapter, we'll talk about how to keep the lines of communication open throughout your dog's life.

Connecting with Your Dog Throughout His Life

"My mom had a terrier/husky mix aptly named Scruffy, and he had an amazing personality. When one of the grandkids had a scraped knee, he'd ever-so-gently lick the wound to heal it. If Mom had a rough day, he'd forego the usual evening romping hour and contentedly lay with his head in her lap. If Gram couldn't get out of the rocker to brush him, he'd snuggle up close to her legs and sit quietly. When the elderly collie who lived next door wanted to play, he'd run along the fence at her speed, and when she died, he howled in mourning.

Scruffy also had a great sense of humor, and he showed it at the most unexpected moments. One time my brother hitched him to a baby sled that held his year-old son, and that dog took off across a field like a shot out of a cannon, with my brother scrambling along behind. When Scruffy stopped and Larry caught up, the baby was squealing with laughter—and so was the dog!"

—Marie N.

Life with a dog is an adventure, to say the least. There will be times when you'll question the sanity of your decision to adopt one, and there also will be other times when you'll wonder how you ever lived without that lovable, fuzzy face.

There is no love like that of a dog, as I'm sure millions of pet owners will attest. There is a quality to that relationship that makes it like no other. Maybe it's because a dog will love you no matter what. A dog's ability to overlook faults and forgive transgressions is legendary. This trait is so embedded in the canine psyche that at times it has caused a great deal of suffering and even death to some dogs. We've all known or read of dogs who died of grief when they lost a beloved owner, canine companion, or other family member. And I personally knew a service dog, a black Lab named Inky, who eventually was kicked to death by his drunken owner, yet he never attempted to defend himself. Always respect this quality in your dog, and never do anything that calls that loyalty into question.

Humans have a lot to learn from the canine species, and living with a dog gives you plenty of opportunities to witness a level of innate goodness that defies comparison. A dog's greatest desire in life is to please the pack leader, and if that leader is you, you are a very lucky person indeed. By being a loving pack leader who deserves respect, you will develop a level of friendship that you are unlikely to find anywhere else.

In addition to these lofty traits, your dog is a perfect example of a being who lives in the present moment. If you're smart, you will pay attention and take notes. Unless they're ill, dogs never pass up the opportunity to feel good and share their happiness—whether it's enjoying the wind flapping their ears, or eating with a gusto unmatched by pie-eating contestants, or running flat out just for the sheer joy of it. Dogs know how to have a great time, and they know how to show and share their enthusiasm. Who can resist someone whose whole body is wagging in excitement?

Dogs also know when to rest and how to do it completely. On any hot day, look for the nearest shady spot, and there will be your dog, on his back, totally spread out, tongue lolling, snoozing comfortably. From his perspective, the only thing that would be better is if he was lying like that in a pool with you next to him!

One thing dogs are not is good liars. They certainly can be mischievous, and they may hedge a bit when you ask them direct questions they don't want to answer, but by and large, you can tell right away when a dog isn't being completely honest. It's so contrary to their nature to be something they're not that it shows immediately in their eyes and posture.

That's not to say they're incapable of having a sense of humor. On the contrary, I've known a number of dogs who absolutely delight in outwitting or playing tricks on other animals or people. Canines certainly have the capability for a wide range of personalities.

Learning to converse with your dog telepathically will add a wonderful new dimension to your friendship. Let's take a look at some of the different stages of canine life and how telepathic communication can help you better understand what's going on.

LIFE WITH A PUPPY

If you bring a puppy into your home, your adventure will begin in a manner very similar to that of most new parents: Expect to spend lots of time and energy tending to your baby's needs, because at this point, that's just what he is. However, remember that this baby is a *dog*, not a human, and that he needs to learn what it means to be a good *dog*. If you start at this early age responding to the real needs of your puppy, you will ensure a much happier life for both of you in the long run.

Think about it like this: Imagine that you adopt a child from another culture with the understanding that you must raise that child to retain her cultural heritage. You would have to learn everything you could about the customs of the land of her birth, and then you would have to do your best to use those same customs in raising her.

This scenario is similar to the one you're in with your puppy. You may think that your dog will be happier living like a human, but that is not the reality. Does this mean you should deny affection or treats or soft beds? Absolutely not. Instead, recognize and meet the basic requirements of a healthy canine psyche first, and then add all the affection and love you have to give. That said, you can begin using telepathy right away to help your puppy adjust to life with you.

Talking to Your Pup

Hopefully, you started your telepathic connection when you met your puppy for the first time. Perhaps you didn't receive a lot of words but had to interpret feelings instead. That's to be expected with a puppy. After all, the little one barely knows dog language, let alone human language! And hopefully you've continued the conversation, both verbally and telepathically.

You can help your puppy learn about the world around him, and what you expect of him, by telling him as you go along. Just as you would with a toddler, keep the information simple and easy to understand. You may want to start with simple exercises such as "lift your front paw" or "follow me." Keep in mind that dogs live in the present moment and that praise or correction needs to take place *immediately*, not even five seconds later—otherwise, he won't know what you're praising or correcting him for. Also remember that at this stage, a lot of repetition is necessary. Be patient! Sometimes it may take weeks for your puppy to understand and remember your message completely.

Pawprint

Remember that dogs live in the present moment. You must praise or correct *immediately*. Otherwise, your puppy won't understand what it's for. This is especially important when housebreaking—harsh words hours after the incident only will cause confusion and fear, so a scolding at this point will not correct the problem. Keep in mind that dogs *want* to please, so they learn better through positive reinforcement than through punishment.

As you teach your puppy what you want him to do—or *not* do—start by clearing your own mind and focusing on the task at hand. Mentally picture him performing the desired action. It's especially important at this stage for you to form clear, *positive* images to transmit to your puppy. Avoid thinking about what you don't want or about what you're afraid he'll do. There is no mental picture for "don't"—if you think "Don't jump up on the sofa," the mental picture is the same as "Jump up on the sofa."

Think about it: If I said to you "Don't think about a rose," the first thing you'd think of would be a rose. Now how would you picture "no rose"? See what I mean? You end up with nothing. (And, by the way, dogs don't understand what that circle with a slash through it means. They discount it as unintelligible.) Instead, clearly see your pup sitting calmly beside the sofa at your feet. This image is clear and easy to understand. Remember this tactic so you can use it with your dog at any age.

Pawprint

Note that there is no mental picture for negatives such as "don't" or "no." Instead of thinking "Don't run away!" think "Come sit by my feet." This works well for dogs at any age.

The Right Way to Say "No"

When your dog is at this age, begin using a specific sound to deter your youngster from unwanted behaviors. A short, forceful "Sshh!" at the moment of correction, used consistently, works better than several different commands, such as "No!" or "Stop!" or "Hey!" or using your puppy's name, which may be confusing.

The idea is to teach not to frighten. Yelling at a dog is not necessary; clear instructions from a confident pack leader are. When you need to correct a behavior, stop after the correction and repeat the mental image of the correct behavior and try again. Keep your training sessions short (10 minute max.) and end on a positive note to build our puppy's self-esteem. Try to use your puppy's name only for positive reasons or to call his attention to you. Otherwise, you will create a negative connotation to the sound of your pup's name, and after you went through the effort of learning what he wanted to be called, that would be a real shame!

THE AWKWARD ADOLESCENT

Depending on your puppy's breed, you may see some odd or unexpected behaviors cropping up at around the one-year mark. Even if you've had him neutered (and please do—the last thing we need are more unwanted puppies to euthanize!), there still are hormonal changes that can occur and cause your sweet puppy to act suddenly like a maniacal teenager.

If you started off on the right paw with training and telepathic conversation, you'll find this period much easier to handle. Remember that it is only a phase—eventually it will pass. However, it is most important that you continue your training regimen and maintain your role as benevolent pack leader throughout your dog's adolescence. Otherwise, you may end up with a dominant, aggressive adult.

Note that *everyone* in your household—even children—must be in a dominant or pack-leader position over your dog, especially when he's at this age. If anyone in the house is not capable of *gently* getting your dog into a calm, submissive state, now is the time to teach him or her how to do it. The longer you wait to do so, the more difficult it will be, and the more you'll encourage neurotic, aggressive behaviors. Refer to Chapter 3 for reminders, if necessary.

Continue to talk with your dog verbally and telepathically. At this stage, there should be more feedback from your dog, so start spending more time listening to allow more of a two-way communication to develop. Begin to ask more complex questions, as well as those that relate to how your dog feels or what he wants. You may not always like what you hear during this period, but at least you will know what your friend is thinking and feeling, and you can use this information to guide you.

ARRIVING AT ADULTHOOD

If you've had your dog since puppyhood, your telepathic bond should be well developed, and you no doubt are able to have regular conversations with your dog. The most important thing I can say is this: Remember to listen! So often we think we know what our human family members are going to say, or think, or feel, that we don't really have two-way conversations—they're more like lectures. It's easy to fall into the same trap with our canine family members, assuming that we already "know" what they're going to say or ignoring what we don't want to hear. Living with someone doesn't mean that you live inside his or her head, and loving doesn't necessarily mean that you always understand what's going on inside there.

Doggie Diaries

When Larry brought home a fuzzy golden retriever/Lab mix puppy, his children were four and seven. The kids loved the little guy and named him "Luke Yardwalker." The puppy quickly became a much-loved member of the family, accompanying them on camping trips, long hikes on the Appalachian Trail, and just about everywhere else.

As Luke grew, his loving and gentle personality endeared him to everyone in the family, but he seemed to have a special relationship with their daughter Megan. By the time she was five, it became clear that she was communicating telepathically with Luke. For instance, before Luke would even beg for a treat, Megan would say, "Mom, Luke says he wants a treat." (Note that she didn't just say, "Luke wants a treat.") Fortunately, her parents never made her feel that her ability wasn't real. Much to their credit, Megan's conversations were taken at face value, and she continued to contribute Luke's perspective in situations involving him. Not surprisingly, they still have a special bond to this day.

The moral of the story is this: The ability to telepathically communicate with animals is natural, and many children, if they are not conditioned out of it, are able to do it easily. Use this knowledge to your advantage, and include your children in your communication sessions with your dog. Encourage them to nurture this ability and to use it as an aid in training and caring for their pet.

—From Danika's Casebook

At this point, your dog's personality is well developed, and you've no doubt had plenty of opportunities to experience the normal ups and downs of any relationship. You probably have a good idea of your dog's likes and dislikes and have seen his sense of humor, fits of temper, mischievousness, happiness, sadness, illness, and the whole gamut of feelings. Each experience is an opportunity for you to hone your communication skills and learn a little more about your furry friend.

You may find that some issues will keep recurring: a certain behavior problem or a common complaint such as separation anxiety. These present opportunities for improvement in your relationship. Ask your dog to tell you what's going on from his perspective—you may be surprised or disappointed by what you hear, but use the information to make your lives happier.

Separation Anxiety

Let's take that thorny issue of separation anxiety. You already know that your dog is a pack animal and feels better and safer when he's with his pack. A simple solution to this problem is to maintain a conversation with your dog as you leave the house, giving details of where you are going, why he can't come with you, and approximately when you'll return. Even after you are on the road, you can continue the conversation, answering his concerns as you go.

It's not necessary (or safe) to be in a meditative state every time you speak with your dog. As you've become more adept at telepathic communication, it will probably seem more like having a chat with someone who's sitting inside your head. Just as with conversations you have with humans, there are some times when you will want to give your dog your undivided, solemn attention and other times when a less focused approach is okay.

If you plan to be away for an extended period—say, for a business trip—prepare your dog for your absence by telling him about the trip as soon as you know you will be taking it. Explain as much as you can, and address any fears or questions he may have. While you're away, maintain contact when you can—for example, each night when you go to bed, spend a few minutes contacting your friend at home or in the boarding kennel, and visualize the golden cord connecting your hearts. Reassure him that you are thinking of him and miss him, and that you will be home as you promised.

These might seem like insignificant conversations to you, but when you're the one left at home, they can be the most important part of your day.

ROOM FOR ONE MORE?

Perhaps you've found yourself thinking about adding another pet to the household. One of the most common reasons people consider getting a second dog is to provide company for the first dog while they're at work or away. You might think that having two dogs would mean double the work, but in some ways, it makes your life a little easier.

For instance, although you will be paying to feed and maintain two mouths instead of one, the increased attention and companionship that your first dog receives may eliminate some of the more destructive behaviors that are caused by boredom and loneliness. Note, however, that the decision to invite another animal to join the family is just as important as the first decision to adopt a dog. Take your time, and be sure that the decision is right for your family and life situation.

Now that you are an animal communicator, you have the ability to gather information from an excellent source: your current canine companion. He should be the first family member you consult when you consider adopting another pet. After all, who's going to be left alone with the new one all day, every day?

For instance, if you have a dog that's firmly convinced that there should be only one pet in the house and that he's it, then you'll have nothing but trouble if you try to alter that situation. On the other hand, if your dog craves constant companionship, he absolutely might love to have a playmate.

It's also possible that your dog is a "cat person" and would prefer feline company instead of another canine. (Or perhaps a ferret, bird, or rabbit.) Don't laugh! A friend of mine had a sweet male Sheltie who adopted a feral mother cat and five kittens—he worried over them and protected them, and he even shared his food with them once they were admitted to the house.

Doggie Diaries

Multispecies, multipet households can be a lot of fun. The old adage about fighting like cats and dogs doesn't always hold true. In fact, if the animals are raised together in a loving, attentive family, there's no reason that even species that are supposed to be enemies couldn't live together happily.

I've done consultations with families who have various combinations of dogs, cats, birds, reptiles, ferrets, rabbits, etc., and found that large families are more likely to have multiple pets. Perhaps each child wants a specific breed or species, or perhaps the fact that there's already a crowd means that one more isn't as noticeable.

Sometimes there are difficulties—one of the brood doesn't get along with another—but, in general, these situations seem to be happy. (Chaotic at times but happy.) The greatest caution I can give is always to use common sense. If there are known antagonists or if past altercations have occurred, there always should be supervision when the adversaries interact. Also, be particularly cautious when one species has a distinct size or speed advantage, especially when a new critter is introduced to the existing clan. Even with the best precautions, accidents will sometimes happen. Before issuing punishment in these cases, be sure that you have the facts.

For example, a friend's Doberman, Indie, generally got along fine with the family's group of birds, whether they were in or out of their cages. However, one green Jenday conure named Max had a habit of swooping down on the unsuspecting dog and teasing her.

Usually the birds were out of their cages only when the family was present, but one day Max was mistakenly left out while the kids went outside to play. When Indie wasn't watching, Max plunged down and pecked at her heels. Instinctively, the Doberman turned and snapped, and unfortunately caught the little bird right in her jaws, killing him instantly.

Poor Indie was shocked, ashamed, and distraught over the mishap, as was the rest of the family. This clearly was not an incident of murderous intent but an accident of surprise and strength over fragility. It took a while for the whole tragic incident to be forgiven and forgotten, but you can be sure that the birds and dog have been more attentively supervised since this incident.

—From Danika's Casebook

Introducing Your New Dog

Once you have decided that there's room for one more, repeat the steps you used previously for finding the right dog (or cat, or bird, but let's assume for now that it's a dog). It's just as important to begin with a good relationship with the new dog as it is to maintain the excellent relationship you have with your current dog.

Tell the new pet that he will be joining a household that already has a dog, and make sure that this is acceptable to him. Address any concerns that come up, whether from you, your family, your dog, or the new pet. If you do so *before* the adoption takes place, you will help to make the transition pleasant for everyone.

When you're ready to bring the new dog home, remember to take a long walk together before coming into the house. Have a telepathic conversation as you go, answering questions and calming any anxieties. Once you've bonded with each other, you can have your current dog join you on your walk. This allows the two dogs to meet on neutral territory, with you firmly in their minds as pack leader.

The dogs naturally will jockey for position in the pack, but if you are a calm, assertive leader who shows no favoritism, you will be able to smooth over any disagreements that may occur. Be aware of your own tendencies to dote on the new dog or to favor your first dog, and avoid both situations. Either one will encourage strife between the two dogs, which may result in such behaviors as fighting and aggressiveness, or anxiety and nervousness. The goal is to have the dogs coexist happily as calm, submissive members of your pack.

If you continue to have regular conversations with your pack members, you will find it easy to deal with issues as they arise, before they can grow into larger problems. Communicating regularly will create the strongest possible bond between you and all your pets, and you'll find that all of you derive even more pleasure from the relationship.

This advice works just as well if you are bringing a different species into the house as the second (or third or fourth) pet. Of course, you're not going to take a cat or a bird for a long walk, but if at all possible, have the first meeting between your current dog and the new pet occur on neutral territory. Doing so will avoid triggering your dog's natural defensive tendencies. Again, be sure to assert your position as pack leader. Combine this understanding of the canine psyche with telepathic communication to help everyone get introduced and get along.

Now it's time to talk about how you can deepen your emotional bond with your dog even more. Let's head on to the next chapter and get started!

Deepening Your Emotional Bond

"Life before Skip was okay. I had a job I liked,
good friends, and a generally happy existence.
But there's no comparison to life with Skip. I can't
imagine how I ever lived without that dog! My life is
so much richer and more meaningful by just having
Skip with me. Everything that I enjoyed before
is just magnified by the amazing, joyous way he is.
Whether it's playing Frisbee or just lounging on the
couch, my little Skippy whippet is a constant
reminder of living each moment to its fullest. And
he's a living, breathing example of unconditional
love and faithfulness. I find that I'm a much better
human because of Skip's influence."

—Jamie K.

Once you've had a canine friend, your life is never the same again. A dog's natural way of being—loving, loyal, and honest—is hard to find anywhere else. The ability to live in the present moment also is a great lesson for humans, who seem to be addicted to living in either the past or the future.

Millions and millions of people have lived with dogs, and some have learned these lessons better than others. But most have not had the benefit of using animal communication to deepen their relationship with their dogs—imagine how much better yours will be simply by using the skills you've gained so far!

Continue to build and strengthen your relationship with your dog just by having regular conversations with him. Practice, practice, practice your skills—test yourself with other pets and animals, get feedback from other communicators, and keep notes for yourself so you can validate what you receive and build confidence in your ability. Lots of people talk to their dogs, but few actually have conversations, as you've learned to do. The key is to keep it up throughout your dog's life and to have it be as normal as talking to another human being.

FOREVER FRIENDS

Whether you start out with a puppy or with an older dog, as you spend time with your canine friend, you'll get to know all the nuances of personality that make your dog unique. You also will learn from your communications with other animals that each one is an individual, with distinct personality traits. Don't confuse these traits with breed characteristics, which refer to appearance, temperament, and breed behavior. For example, by nature of their breed, German shepherds look a particular way, are generally more serious than other dogs, and tend to make excellent guards.

Before selecting a dog, you probably did some research on different breeds and their standard characteristics. The role a particular breed was created to fill certainly will affect its overall disposition, and learning about these characteristics will help you narrow your choice and avoid mistaken assumptions. For instance, if you're a couch potato, you might do better with a greyhound than with a Jack Russell terrier—something that may not seem apparent at first, but would be revealed in your research.

By contrast, personality traits are not breed-specific but dog-specific. In any group of dogs, just as in any group of people, there will be a variety of personalities. You'll find some who are more withdrawn, some who are more sociable, some who are more submissive, and some who are more assertive. These variations make each one unique. Let's use our German shepherd example: Although many German shepherds are seriously hard workers, Fritz is a big goof. He has the intelligence of his breed, but he is very gregarious with strangers and would not be happy as a guard dog. Likewise, Maddie, a Jack Russell terrier, is more standoffish than most of her breed, and she would sooner lie in the sun and watch rabbits than chase them. Fritz and Maddie are not bad dogs; they simply are who they are.

Knowing your own dog's personality traits will help you know the best ways to strengthen your bond. If Maddie were your dog, you might decide that trips to the beach would be more fun than trying to get her to participate in agility trials. You also might find, however, if you *really* wanted to do agility and were willing to work within her tolerances, that Maddie would comply as much as she could just to make you happy.

By also knowing your own personality traits, you will help your relationship with your pup, because you'll better understand how your personalities mesh or where there may be sticking points. If you are a high-powered individual used to getting your own way and almost demanding personal contact with others, you may inadvertently overwhelm and frighten a timid dog like Flyer, a retired greyhound. Once you know that Flyer loves physical contact but prefers to initiate it, you might alter the way you approach her and allow her to come to you after you've settled in your chair rather than rushing up to her to rub her head.

Dogs have an amazing desire to "fit in" with their pack. Bonnie Bergin, EdD, founder of Canine Companions for Independence and author of *Understanding "Dog Mind,"* calls this "synchronizing." She says that if you understand how humans and dogs interact and mesh, you can shape your dog's personality to fit yours without breaking his spirit. She asserts that this synchrony between human and canine, with things slightly in the human's favor as leader, makes an ideal relationship.

Mark This Spot!

For a more in-depth discussion of human and canine personality traits and some excellent information about educating both yourself your dog, see *Understanding "Dog Mind,"* by Bonnie Bergin, EdD. In the chapter on personality, you'll find a remarkably simple system for determining which of four general personality types you and your dog match most closely. Although we're all a blending of the four, each of us falls into one type more often than into any of the others. Knowing which one fits best will enable you to assess which tactics will work best for you or your dog in each situation. This knowledge greatly eases training, shaping, and bonding, which makes life more enjoyable for both of you.

I like Dr. Bergin's philosophy because, like the philosophy of dog behavior consultant Cesar Millan, it acknowledges the validity of the dog's own personality and gives you tools to help you meet your dog's needs while meeting your own. Dogs have a right to be who they are, just as you and I do. By being as diligent about learning their traits and behaviors as they are about learning ours, we are better able to ensure that the signals we give line up with our intent—that is, that we're not inadvertently sending mixed messages or the wrong message. This makes for better communication and fewer misunderstandings.

Mark This Spot!

A good way to strengthen your connection with your canine friend for life is to participate in the American Kennel Club's Canine Good Citizen (CGC) Program. The AKC developed this two-part program to emphasize responsible pet ownership and basic good manners for dogs. CGC is a good first step in the training process. It enhances your bond and lays the foundation for participation in other activities. Dogs enjoy training; it provides mental stimulation, a feeling of accomplishment, and an avenue for spending quality time together.

Since 1989, CGC has been used in a variety of situations, including screening for therapy work, dealing with problem dogs, and helping children learn to train their pets. Its expanding use is having an impact in the larger community, as issues of responsible dog ownership have come under scrutiny. The CGC program tests dogs and their owners in ten basic areas, which include such things as good manners with strangers, proper walking behavior, interacting with other dogs, appearance and grooming, and basic commands. To learn more about how your dog can be a Canine Good Citizen, check out the website: www.akc.org/events/cgc/index.cfm, or look for the book, *The Canine Good Citizen: Every Dog Can Be One*, by Jack and Wendy Volhard.

We can use dogs' natural ability to read and understand our facial expressions, body language, and tonal qualities to enhance their lives by giving clear and consistent information about what's expected of them as pack members. This gift is one of the greatest we can give to our dogs: loving guidance with a clear purpose that provides a secure place within the pack. This sense of security lets a dog know that you are a forever friend.

Doggie Diaries

Eli was a shy, ten-year-old boy who kept to himself, happily sitting for hours figuring out the mechanical workings of the toys he'd take apart. He was very intelligent, but he lacked the social skills of other children his age.

Butterscotch also was a bit shy, although not as much as Eli. The two-year-old golden retriever had been through a tough time with her first family, where she was mostly ignored. When they moved, they callously dumped her at a shelter, where she stole the heart of Gretchen, a volunteer who also happened to be Eli's mom.

From the day Eli and Butterscotch met, it was a match made in heaven. The two bonded quickly and were soon inseparable, which delighted both Gretchen and Peter, Eli's dad. Butterscotch was a bit more outgoing than Eli, so she was able to draw him out of his shell and give him a reason to interact with other kids. She also was intelligent, but Eli had a more assertive personality, so she only occasionally challenged his lead—just enough to keep him on his toes. The combination of the two personalities was just about perfect, and it often was said that either one would do anything for the other.

As they grew up together, it became clear that Butterscotch was a consistently good influence on Eli. Gone was the loner who avoided social situations. Although he would never be a social butterfly, Eli expanded his horizons and got involved in Boy Scouts. He took Butterscotch with him to meetings and campouts whenever he could, and after receiving many compliments about their wonderful relationship, he asked his mom whether they could begin therapy-dog training as part of a Scout project.

Gretchen and Peter quickly agreed, and the boy and the dog diligently worked through the necessary courses. Within a short time, Butterscotch and Eli received therapy dog and handler certification and began weekly visits to local nursing homes and hospital wards. The team was a hit wherever they went. They were the perfect combination of calm confidence and intelligent interest that drew the patients out and made them feel comfortable.

Theirs is a beautiful example of how well dog and human behavior can mesh and, in doing so, enhance the quality of life for both.

—From Danika's Casebook

KEEPING IN TOUCH

You already know that you don't have to be in the same room to talk to your dog. In fact, sometimes telepathy works better at a distance, when you can't physically see your dog and anticipate his response based on body language. Use this knowledge to enhance your relationship. When you take your lunch break at work, go for a walk outside, or sit quietly and talk to your dog, letting him know you're thinking about him or reminding him that you'll take him to the dog park when you get home. Ask how the day's going, or how he feels, or whether he's keeping an eye on things at the house.

If you have to go on a trip without your dog, use the same method to stay in touch while you're gone. Assure your dog that you miss him, and that you think about him often. Ask how he's faring while you're away, and let him know when you'll be back. Even if you are extremely busy during the day, take a few moments before bed to connect with your dog.

You can have conversations at any time of the day, even for a few minutes at a time, and, unlike other friendly exchanges, you don't have to use the phone! After a while, you may find that your connection with your dog is so easy and fluent that you can get reports on what's going on at the house or prevent an "accident" by checking in to see whether it's okay for you to stop at the store on the way home.

There have been people whose pets alerted them to come home because a fire had started, or because another pet was in danger, or simply because they had run out of food or water. By constantly building your connection with your dog, you attune yourself to hear more messages more clearly.

DOG DREAMS

There is another way that you and your dog may communicate: in the dream world. Just as people you know and love may appear in your dreams, so may your dog. Pay attention to these dreams! Your dog's spirit may use this avenue because you haven't received the message any other way.

I am not a big fan of books and manuals of dream interpretation, because we each create our own dream world, and we are the only ones who can accurately interpret it. These books may be fun to read, and it's certainly possible that many people understand certain symbols the same way. However, the problem with these books is that they assume that such symbols mean the same thing for everyone, or that there is only one "right" way of interpreting them. At this point, these books become limiting, and you actually may misinterpret your own dreams. We don't really know what others are thinking or what shapes their attitudes and beliefs, so I find it hard to believe that we can accurately interpret symbols for each other.

I prefer to follow the "way of the adventurer" as taught by Serge Kahili King, PhD, Hawaiian Kahuna shaman and author of *Urban Shaman*. This method suggests that any time you don't understand a dream's meaning or what a character is trying to say, you go back into the dream and replay it, so that you can understand it or simply ask the characters and symbols what they're trying to say. This is so similar to our method of telepathic communication that it should be easy to see how it can work for you.

EXERCISE 8

Dream Interpretation

Because dreams free our subconscious from the constraints we unconsciously place on it, they can tell us a lot about ourselves and our world. They're also a great avenue of communication for our dogs. (As you know if you're a dog owner, dogs have very vivid dreams as well!) If you've had a dream about your dog, this exercise will help you interpret it and see whether he or she is trying to send you a message.

Here's how to do it:

1. If your dog appears to you in a dream, and you don't understand why, try to have a telepathic conversation with your dog while you're awake to see whether you can get clarification. It's possible that your dog's spirit is trying to communicate directly with your spirit, so your dog may not be consciously aware of a message.

2. If this is the case, lie down in a comfortable spot where you won't be disturbed—if possible, wherever you had the dream. Close your eyes and center yourself. Then calmly state your intent to return to the dream world, to that specific dream, to find its meaning.

3. Slowly recall the dream in as much detail as you can, adding more details as they come to you. Try to be as conscious of your inner space as possible, as you did in the Sacred Clearing exercise (page 37).

4. When your dog appears, pay close attention to what's going on and to any messages you may hear. If you don't understand what's happening or what your dog is saying, ask him or her for clarification, saying that you want to understand. (You also can do this with any character or symbol in your dream.)

5. If necessary, go through the steps again until you feel confident that you got the message. You even may wish to ask your Spirit Guide to join you to help you interpret what you see and hear. (See page 39 for more on finding and reaching your Spirit Guide.) Sometimes you can get better information if you try on separate occasions, writing down as much as you remember each time and then comparing your notes.

6. You may find another suggestion of Serge King's helpful: Continue the dream. That is, stay in the dream past the point where it stopped before, and watch what happens. Are you creating the new ending? Of course! Feel free to do so—it may give you an even better explanation. Because you created the dream in the first place, you can't be wrong—your Inner Self has the answers.

7. If you frequently have dreams that need interpretation, try keeping a notebook and pen near your bed. When you wake up, immediately write down everything you remember. Sometimes the most vivid dreams are the ones right before you wake up, and they're usually the quickest to fade from memory.

Visits from Beyond

You may experience another type of dog dream if you have a pet who has crossed over. I discuss communicating with your deceased pet in more detail in Chapter 12 (see page 185), but I will mention here that sometimes pets who have passed away will attempt to contact you in the dream world.

There may be a number of reasons for this. If the dream occurs soon after your dog has crossed, it's most likely that your dog misses you and the physical contact and is attempting to maintain it. Many dogs stay close to their families for a period of time before continuing their journey.

Your dog also may appear in your dream as a guardian or guide. Some pets decide to remain in spirit form indefinitely and to keep close watch on the family from that vantage. These spirit dogs become almost like guardian angels. If your dog has chosen this path, then you may feel his presence at times, especially during periods of stress.

Sometimes your spirit dog will appear in your dreams to give you comfort—or a warning. Pay attention as much as possible to the context and details of these dreams, for they may provide you with guidance from your friend. If you are not sure that you have received the message clearly, use the technique you learned in Exercise 8 to get clarification.

Doggie Diaries

I recently did a communication for a woman who had three dogs on the other side, one of whom, Toby, had crossed over fairly recently. Donna said that she had been seeing Toby in her dreams and wondered if it meant he was coming back soon.

When I tried to tune into him, I kept getting a very vivid image of all three dogs standing in a triangle around Donna's husband, Bill, who had been chronically ill for some time. It was clear that the dogs were concerned about Bill's health and were conveying to me the message that if he didn't make some serious changes very quickly, he would cross over soon. The dogs were doing what they could to protect and heal him, but it would not be enough if he didn't act himself.

I relayed this message and was told that Bill was indeed neglecting his health, much to Donna's frustration and dismay. She believed that Bill would listen to the warning, and we both hoped that it would be enough to change his attitude.

This is a prime example of the kind of connection you can make with your dog. When you put in the effort, you are repaid not only with love and loyalty in this lifetime but with a bond that continues beyond.

—*From Danika's Casebook*

We'll discover even more ways to strengthen the relationship between you and your dog in Chapter 7 by learning to deal with behavioral difficulties in ways that create understanding and growth not separation. Let's go there now!

Ain't Misbehavin'

*"I did everything I could to let him know that
I wanted to please him, but somehow, he never
understood me. I could never figure out what he
wanted me to do or how to understand him."*

—Jake, collie mix,
about his previous owner

I'm going to go out on a limb and say that I believe that misbehavior in your dog almost is always due to misunderstanding and miscommunication from the pack leader...that is, *you*. Dogs are honest in their behavior. As a rule, they do not set out intentionally to do something bad; they simply do what they feel like doing at that moment. Unless they have been given clear and consistent instruction about the behavior that's expected of them, they will continue to decide on their own what's the best thing to do.

It's a sad statement about human beings that we expect canines to understand our language instinctively, and yet we rarely make any attempt to learn theirs. Many—if not most—cases in which dogs are given up because of bad behavior are really due to plain ignorance on the part of the owners. In other words, they have little or no understanding of how a dog's mind works.

Doggie Diaries

Recently, I met a woman at the supermarket who started to tell me about the new black Lab her family had just gotten from a shelter. The dog was about two years old, and they'd had her about two weeks. During that time, she had destroyed furniture, peed on the carpet, and was totally rambunctious and out of control around the family.

The woman said she resorted to crating the dog for the entire work day, and her husband's solution was either to return her to the SPCA or to use physical violence to force the dog to behave. She topped this off by saying, "She's nothing like our last Lab—she was so quiet and good! That's why we wanted another one."

My first question to the woman was this: "How old was your first Lab when you got her?" She responded, "Oh, we got her when she was eight weeks old—what an adorable puppy." I said it sounded like they were expecting their old dog in a new body and ventured that not all Labs are exactly the same.

This new dog already was two years old, was taken from her family for a reason she didn't understand, and was still adjusting to this upheaval in her life. In addition, her new owners had no idea how she was treated before or what the circumstances of her life had been up to that point. It could take some time for her to get over her past traumas. Keeping her in a crate all day only added to her boredom and frustration. It did nothing to cure her "bad" behavior—it only worsened it. This situation required patience and understanding on the part of the family. Physical and mental abuse only teach a dog to be afraid of you. I urged her to get some help on how to help this dog or to think about returning her.

When I saw the woman again, she said she had started taking the Lab for long walks in the morning before work, which seemed to help with the destructive behavior—the dog was too tired to destroy things. I also gave the woman some behavior training resources to try. Hopefully the Lab and her new family are getting along better now.

—From Danika's Casebook

Unfortunately, the example of the poor Lab in "The Doggie Diaries" on page 113 is not uncommon. So many people still have this out-dated notion that dogs are no different than any other possession—that one dog is like any other dog, and that all dogs should behave predictably. If that's what you think, you'd be better off with a stuffed dog—your life will be much easier, and you won't be needlessly traumatizing a living, breathing creature who has feelings and needs of his own.

UNDERSTANDING "DOG SPEAK"

In Chapter 3, I mentioned that learning a little bit about dog psychology could improve greatly your relationship with your dog. Understanding that a dog is happiest when he or she has a strong, *loving* pack leader to follow is a major step forward in human–canine relations. The next step in increasing understanding between the species is learning the canine language.

Your ability to communicate telepathically with your dog will do wonders for addressing problems as they arise. As you talk to your dog more frequently, and the communication becomes truly two-way, you probably will find that problems are increasingly minor and easily solved.

In the beginning, however, I find that it is very helpful to have a basic knowledge of how canines communicate among themselves. Dogs are extremely social animals who have developed an extensive language that is almost completely nonverbal. Dogs communicate by scent first, then by sight, and then by sound.

Communicating by Scent

The canine sense of smell is legendary. Dogs have better olfactory recognition and recollection by far than any other mammal. They have more than 100 times the olfactory receptors humans do: their 280 million receptors fill up to 20 square inches of the olfactory mucosa, while our 20 million cover barely half an inch. When they're born, puppies are blind, but their noses function immediately, and their sense of smell is their primary means of gathering information about the world around them, and it remains so for the rest of their lives.

Dogs communicate with their sense of smell in much the same way we do with written texts. An author speaks directly to the reader through visual symbols such as words, photos, and diagrams, even though the two never meet face-to-face. Dogs transmit similar volumes of information to each other through scents left by marking with their urine, feces, and glands. What dog owner hasn't seen their dog thoroughly inspect a well-marked hydrant or pole? These are the canine kiosks of the neighborhood; in a few minutes, your dog learns about the social and physical goings-on of every other canine who left a calling card, and adds his or own unique message to the "bulletin board."

This ability to detect and recall even minute levels of scent is what enables a bloodhound to track a person even when the trail is four days old, or tells your own pup which particular stick you threw into the woods. It also plays a big part in how your dog relates to you and others.

We unknowingly communicate with our dogs through our bodies' odors all the time—if we are afraid, for example, they can smell it in our sweat. Think about meeting a dog for the first time: You generally are greeted with a wet nose testing the air, or your hands, or your privates, or wherever else a scent can be found. This gives the dog the most information about you, and because of the amazing way a dog's olfactory system is designed, this information will be permanently stored in his or her memory. You can use this to your advantage in solving some behavior issues. For example, if you are trying to acclimate your dog to sleeping in his own bed, put something you've worn or used, but not washed, in the bed. Your comforting scent may help the transition go more smoothly.

Humans are affected strongly by scent as well, although our noses are not nearly as developed as canines'. Unlike dogs, however, who revel in the smells of the natural world, humans spend much of their time and a great deal of cash trying to hide most scents with even stronger ones. This penchant for perfume is often distasteful to dogs, who would much rather smell the "real you." They also may have strong respiratory reactions to heavily scented perfumes, cleaners, air fresheners, and such; be wary of over-using such items in your house.

Communicating by Sight

The second form of communication used by dogs is sight, which manifests in a range of facial expressions, body postures, and movements. For example, a dog who is alert but not feeling threatened will approach you with ears forward, mouth closed, standing slightly forward on his toes, and with his tail horizontal and slightly wagging.

The same dog would be showing dominance and possibly aggression with some slight changes: the ears are still forward, but the mouth is now open slightly and the teeth are showing; the tail may still wag slightly, but it is now raised and stiff. In this state, the dog is communicating visually that he feels threatened by something but is confident that he can handle the challenge. He is warning that he will defend himself if necessary.

Canine eye contact is another visual cue that humans often misinterpret. In Western culture, eye contact is desirable; in fact, we tend to mistrust someone who will not meet our eyes during conversation. In canine culture, eye contact for more than two or three seconds is considered a sign of dominance or perhaps even impending attack. Some dogs will use an intent stare to make demands or to establish dominance with their owners. With a strong-willed dog, you may need to stare him down and give a low "No!" command; with a less dominant personality, turning away and perhaps yawning will be enough of a signal to stop.

It is wise to teach your dog not to stare, especially if you are raising a puppy, because this behavior may not be well received by canines you meet in public. If your dog seems to pick fights with other dogs, pay closer attention to his or her level of eye contact when you are out together. While other forms of body language may be easier for you to interpret, it is often the eye contact that initiates a confrontation between two dogs. If you can interrupt a stare, you can often diffuse a situation before it escalates. Often all it takes is a quick tap on the behind or a quick "Shhh!" sound.

If you practice recognizing these subtle differences in body language and eye contact, you can influence greatly the outcome of a chance meeting. Remember that there is a distinct advantage to dogs' using visual cues such as these: It avoids unnecessary physical violence because it is easily understood at a distance.

Humans use body language too, although in many cases we display and read it less consciously, depending more on verbal communication for clarification. For instance, if you walk into a room full of people, you probably will be drawn to a person who is facing you and smiling broadly instead of to one who glances at you over his shoulder. However, if the first person said "Nice to see you" in a sarcastic tone and the second said, "Hey buddy! I'll be right over when I put down this tray," the verbal comments would take precedence over the body language.

Knowing that dogs give body language cues greater value than verbal ones can also help you improve the level of communication with your own dog. For example, towering over your dog while vocally trying to initiate play may not evoke the response you're seeking. But if you try bending at the knees or crouching down first, you'll seem much less threatening and your dog may even respond with her own "play bow." Likewise, many dog lovers greet their dogs by rushing up to them, leaning over top of them, and staring right into their eyes while reaching to pet them. In the dog world, this behavior is a display of dominance and possibly aggression. Although your own dog may tolerate this, especially if you are the confirmed pack leader, other dogs may not accept it as submissively.

Remember that your dog sees you as a member of its pack, and reads your body language as if you were another dog. If you learn canine body language, you will better understand how to use your own body language to communicate with your dog.

Communicating by Sound

The third type of communication dogs use, verbal, is often used in response to other cues. It may be used as an alert, as in barking upon smelling or hearing an intruder, or as a final warning before striking, as in growling or snarling at an aggressively approaching dog. Although some dogs bark or howl to express a desire to be near others—whether out of loneliness or as a sort of "calling all dogs!" announcement—most canine verbal sounds appear to be used for close-proximity communication.

Wolf packs use a wide range of barks, yips, growls, and whines to communicate with each other, especially when gathered together. If you take your dog to a dog park, you have probably seen some of the same types of vocalizations. If you watch closely, you'll see that the sounds are almost always accompanied by a body posture, and it is this that takes precedence for a dog. Just as verbal cues are more important to us, body language is more important to dogs. A growl from a dog in a play bow is an invitation to play; a growl from a dog standing stiff-legged with hackles raised is a warning.

When you speak to your dog, use the tone of your voice to indicate emotion and authority. For canines, a lower tone indicates greater dominance and authority, and a higher tone denotes play, excitement, and happiness. If you want your dog to listen to you and obey your command, speak at a lower tone; if you want to praise your dog, use a higher tone. By using the combination of tone of voice and body language, you'll be more likely to get your message across clearly.

Using Your Knowledge

As you can see, there are similarities and differences in how humans and canines communicate among themselves. Even though we use the same methods, we use them differently. If you take the time to learn the nuances of canine language, you will be light-years ahead in creating a happy relationship with your dog.

You can use even this basic knowledge to your advantage and combine it with your telepathic skills. For example, although humans often depend on verbal speech first, dogs use it last, so it's pointless to call your greyhound over and over while he's chasing a rabbit. However, calmly visualizing your dog returning to you and sitting at your feet, while telepathically asking him to return, may have a better result.

Likewise, even though you'll never have the amazing scent-detection ability that your dog does, you can use this sense to talk to him. For instance, you can smooth the introduction of a new person or animal by bringing something with his scent on it into the house first. This works in reverse as well—if you have to go away and leave your dog behind, leave something with your scent on it to give him comfort while you're gone.

Mark This Spot!

I found these two books to be helpful in learning to read canine facial expressions and body language: *Dog Speak* by Bash Dibra and *How to Speak Dog* by Stanley Coren. Both books give descriptions and illustrations of various facial expressions and body postures and what they mean. *How to Speak Dog* also has an appendix with charts of the most common verbal, visual, and body signals and the human translation and emotions they represent.

HANDLING BEHAVIOR PROBLEMS

Every dog owner has had to face certain basic issues that seem to be a normal part of dog ownership. However, if you spend some time learning about how a dog's mind works and how canines communicate, you probably will find that most of these behavior problems are caused by misunderstanding, and that they can be corrected with a combination of telepathic communication and training that responds to a dog's innate needs.

This is not a manual for training your dog—there are plenty of good books, videos, and classes available for that. However, I do advocate nonviolent, encouragement-based training methods that take a dog's nature and personality into consideration. These methods will help shape your dog into a true companion instead of some kind of robot who serves you out of fear.

I also believe that telepathic communication is an excellent aid to training: You can use it to explain why you want something done and to trade feedback on where improvements are needed. Animal communication helps you and your dog understand each other and lets you use the information to continue to build and strengthen your relationship.

Some dogs are more prone to certain behaviors than others, but most dogs go through stages when behavior problems crop up. Puppyhood and adolescence are two periods when your patience is likely to be tested; fortunately, these phases are fairly short-lived. Other behaviors may appear during times of stress or unusual circumstances. Knowing why your dog is exhibiting a behavior will help you understand the best way to help him change it.

As I mentioned, there are numerous sources of information on how to train your dog. You can find some in the Resources section beginning on page 198, as well as in the books and other sources in the "Mark This Spot!" features throughout this book. Find which method works best for you and learn it. The more compassionate methods focus on understanding basic canine behavior and needs and addressing them first. Doing so allows you to anticipate problems before they occur and paves the way for your dog's eager cooperation in learning the behaviors that please you.

One of the most important needs a dog has is an outlet for energy. As I've said elsewhere, many of the consultations I'm asked to do revolve around bad behavior caused by dogs' boredom and lack of physical exercise. So many issues would disappear if we would just remember that dogs need to be mentally and physically challenged to stay healthy, much as we do!

It's also helpful to remember to look at the big picture: If your dog is generally well behaved, don't lose your temper over one infraction—dogs forget and get confused, too. Be sure that you are being clear and consistent, and that your dog understands what you want. If you are not a confident, dependable leader, it's only natural for your dog to ignore you and attempt to take over. Keep in mind that your dog wants to please you, so positive reinforcement works much better than scolding and punishment.

Doggie Diaries

Jake, the collie mix who gave the quote at the beginning of this chapter, is a good case in point. A man in his early 40's brought Jake home from a pet store when he was about three months old, hoping to fill the loneliness left by his divorce. He had never owned a dog before, and really didn't give the whole process much thought or preparation. He had a demanding job, which left him exhausted at the end of each day. He thought that Jake would be the perfect companion to come home to—a friend to sit quietly beside him while he ate dinner or watched TV before going to bed.

Unfortunately, Jake didn't know that this was his owner's expectation, nor could he have fulfilled it as a three-month-old puppy. Jake was just an energetic, growing pup who needed lots of exercise, discipline, and love. These things that take time, patience, and emotional involvement, and they were things the man could not provide at that time.

The first major problem was housebreaking. Jake was left alone most of the day, and, being a puppy, needed to eliminate several times during the man's work hours. At first, the man kept Jake in the kitchen, but when he got tired of cleaning up the floor, he confined Jake to a crate all day, as punishment, and as a way to get control. Of course, Jake didn't understand this; he only knew that he needed to urinate, and couldn't understand why the man yelled at him when he came home.

This confinement led to the next set of problems: whining, chewing, and barking. As a puppy, Jake had an abundance of energy, and as a collie, he needed plenty of mental stimulation. When the man came home, he was exhausted, and had no desire to take Jake for a walk. As soon as Jake would be released from the crate, he would barrel around the house, barking and jumping wildly. He'd pull at the sofa pillows, play tug of war with the drapes, and generally be a nuisance. If the man put him back in the crate, or into the kitchen, he'd whine continuously, and dig at the doorway.

Although the man made no attempt to train Jake, he expected the dog to somehow understand his commands, and yelled at him constantly for his bad behavior. By the time Jake was eight months old, he was an anxious, neurotic dog, who was starting to show aggressive tendencies, such as an occasional attempt at fear biting.

It was at this point that the man decided that Jake was hopeless, and he took him to the local animal shelter. Jake was devastated at the separation, because although the man was not the perfect owner, he was the only one Jake had ever known.

The happy ending to this story is that Francine, who is trained in animal communication, was looking for a collie to adopt. She heard about Jake from one of the shelter's workers, and she went to check him out. They hit it off, and during their "talk," he told her what had happened. Because Francine had consciously worked through the steps of adopting a dog, she knew that Jake would be a good fit for her and her family once his past behavior issues were addressed.

First Francine consulted a dog trainer familiar with canine psychology for the best ways to handle Jake's past as well as his current behavior problems. Then she adopted Jake, took him home, and spent hours, days, and weeks rehabilitating him. Jake got plenty of exercise playing with Francine's children, going on long daily walks, and taking regular trips to the dog park. Francine took Jake to an obedience class, and they worked a little every day at improving his behavior in the house. Her oldest daughter, Jan, began taking Jake to an agility class, where he soon showed outstanding ability. And the entire family gave him plenty of love and companionship.

Now, at two years of age, Jake is a happy, healthy, well-balanced dog, and a cherished family member.

—From Danika's Casebook

When you're faced with a behavior issue, take the time to calm yourself and have a conversation with your dog first. Do a body scan to check for any medical conditions that may be causing pain or crankiness. Ask to hear your dog's point of view on the behavior and why it's occurring. Once you find out why it's happening, work with your dog to discover a better way to handle the situation.

Mark This Spot!

Another book you may find helpful in your study of the canine language is *Pet Speak,* by the editors of *Pets: Part of the Family* magazine. This book provides good information on understanding how pets communicate with their bodies and voices. It also will help you solve a wide variety of common behavior issues.

Specific Behavior Issues

Here are some common behavior problems and some ideas for reshaping them.

Biting and Chewing

All puppies bite and chew on things, just like babies do. It's partly due to teething, but it's also a way of exploring their world—dogs use their mouths where we might use our hands. Your dog's ancestors depended on their ability to bite and grip their prey to bring it down, and they needed strong jaws and teeth to cut away meat from bones and carry hunks to waiting pups. In other words, biting and chewing are natural canine behaviors, so rather than attempting to rewire your dog's brain, provide appropriate chewing opportunities.

Chewing: If chewing is not due to teething, it may be caused by boredom, anxiety, or a natural need to mouth things, as in retrievers. If your dog suddenly picks up the habit, check in to see if there's something bothering him—has something changed in the household, or has something happened recently that's causing him anxiety?

If boredom is the cause, try adding some more exercise and playtime to the schedule, as well as providing more interesting chew toys. Don't put out too many toys at once, but circulate a few at a time. Try "marking" toys with your scent by rubbing them between your hands—this provides some satisfaction for the dog who chews your favorite sneakers because he likes your scent. You also can make a simple tug-of-war toy in the yard: Securely tie an old towel or sheet around a sturdy tree trunk and put a large knot at the end. Now your pup can pull to his heart's content without dislocating your shoulder!

Biting: Biting is a little different in that it is sometimes used as an aggressive or defensive tactic, even during play. Teach your puppy early on that biting is not acceptable by responding with a high-pitched yelp followed immediately by ceasing all attention and ignoring him for a minute or two. This method also works with older dogs. During play time, be sure to take frequent breaks to avoid overstimulation, which often leads to biting. Because dogs crave our attention, giving them a time-out gets the message across quickly: "If I bite, I lose."

Also be conscious of your dog's body language at all times: Many bites occur because the human doesn't understand the visual warning signs. If your dog suddenly becomes aggressive, it may be due to an injury or illness. Sometimes it's triggered by a feeling of being threatened, or possibly it's fear of losing food or status within the family pack.

If you are not firmly established as pack leader, your dog will try to assume that role and may display aggressive behavior when challenged. Again, use a combination of techniques—telepathic communication, behavior shaping, and training—to alter a behavior like this.

Digging

Digging is another typical canine behavior that often is seen as destructive. However, it's just as natural as chewing for some dogs, and likewise it may be caused by boredom and lack of exercise. Digging may become an issue for terriers especially, because they are bred to follow prey into underground tunnels. That job often requires digging, so your dog is just following instinct. To satisfy this instinctual need and save your yard, simply provide a place where it's okay for your dog to dig.

Doggie Diaries

Fred is a retired landscape designer. Gardening has been both a lifelong hobby and his life's work, and now that he has the time, he enjoys spending long hours working in his yard with Dexter, a scrappy terrier mix, at his side. Dexter is a lovable dog and a great companion now, but he and Fred had to work through a big problem: Dexter loves to dig, anywhere, any time.

This compulsion was not something that was discerned easily at the shelter where Fred found Dexter; it became apparent only after they'd bonded through the winter and Fred started his spring gardening tasks. Dexter found the soft, pliable dirt in the flower beds just *perfect* for digging huge holes to crawl into, and if he came across some roots, well, all the better for tugging and pulling!

Dexter's behavior caused Fred more than a little aggravation. Although he loved the little dog, he also loved his garden and wanted to enjoy both. Locking Dexter inside while he was in the yard didn't work: The terrier just barked his head off to get outside. Keeping him tied up in the yard was no better. It seemed that no matter what Fred tried, Dexter's obsession just wouldn't let up.

During a consultation, I discovered that Dexter had no idea why Fred was so upset. He dug in the dirt all the time, but then he'd get mad if Dexter did the same thing. He had tried again and again to help Fred, but every time, he'd get yelled at, or put inside, or tied up. He just didn't understand.

When I relayed this information to Fred, a light bulb went on, and he came up with his own solution: Train Dexter to dig on command! We explained the idea to Dexter, and he was excited and ready to cooperate.

Soon afterward, Fred began working with Dexter on a leash, taking him to a pile of dirt in the yard where it was safe to dig. He spent about a week training Dexter to understand "Dig!" and "Stop!" while using praise and positive reinforcement whenever Dexter correctly followed his command.

Once he could control with confidence where and when Dexter would dig, Fred graduated him to the flower beds, off leash. Now Dexter's natural skill came in handy, especially when there were some small roots to be cleared. Because Dexter now felt useful and had an appropriate avenue for his natural compulsion, he stopped digging holes where he wasn't supposed to and became a very good gardener's helper.

This is an excellent example of how you can change your dog's "misbehavior" into helpful behavior by improving your understanding of how your needs can mesh with his and being creative with your solutions.

—From Danika's Casebook

Barking

Barking is another behavior that often causes problems. As you might expect, dogs bark for a number of reasons, ranging from protecting territory to showing excitement to expressing separation anxiety. These reasons make complete sense to the dog, but they sometimes can be annoying to you and your neighbors.

Once again, understanding the underlying cause is the first step in correcting the behavior. If your dog barks at the mail carrier's approach, he sees it as performing his job as guardian of the household. It's possible to teach your dog that the mail carrier is not a threat, and that you expect him to show manners when someone who is not a threat approaches the house. Being clear about what you expect, by intention and by instruction, and then rewarding good behavior will go a long way toward achieving this goal.

If your dog is barking because of separation anxiety, you have to take a different approach. Not only is the reason different, but the barking generally happens when you're away. Here again, begin by talking with your dog to ascertain the source of his fear. He obviously doesn't like being separated from you, but you also can't take him everywhere you go. It's also likely that his anxiety actually begins before you leave the house, when you pick up your keys or grab your coat.

Start changing this behavior by desensitizing your dog to the triggers—pick up your keys and jingle them, or take your coat out of the closet several times a day without actually leaving. Follow up by assuring him that you will return, and then leave for brief periods. It may be helpful to have someone stay behind to praise him when he remains calm while you're gone. (Warning: If you or your partner pat or reward him in an effort to quiet the barking, you only will reinforce the behavior.) Gradually lengthen the time you're gone, and reinforce your wish for him to be quiet by talking to him telepathically.

Also, don't make a big production out of leaving—say something simple, like, "I'll be back, be a good girl." Be brief and consistent, and leave it at that. The more fawning you do before you leave, the more he'll fear that you're not coming back; otherwise, why would you make such a big deal out of it?

Begging

Begging is a behavior that can be measured in degrees, and the point at which it becomes annoying is a matter of personal preference. Some people find it cute when their dog sits with soulful eyes staring longingly at their plate, hoping for the tiniest morsel to be tossed his way; others can't tolerate the idea of a moochin' pooch.

This behavior is an indicator of how far we've taken dogs from their natural behavior patterns. In wolf packs, only puppies beg, and then only for food; adults either take what they want, or get reprimanded for trying. Humans have encouraged canine begging in two ways: first, we tend to treat our dogs like babies their entire lives, and second, we are their only resource for food, exercise, entertainment, and affection.

Don't blame your dog if he or she is a top-notch beggar; this has happened because he or she has found a method that works—namely, bug you until you respond appropriately! The only way to end this behavior is to stop giving in to your dog's demands. Now there's no need to be heartless; but you do need to be firm. You can alter your behavior and your dog's at the same time. Stop giving handouts. If you're dog is looking for food, make feeding times the same every day, and give lots of praise and some extra attention when your dog has waited patiently. If your dog is seeking attention, focus on devoting a little extra time each day for quality doggie-time, at regular times. Provide what your dog is seeking, but on your terms, and reinforce this by ignoring *your* dog when begging occurs.

Doggie Diaries

Gyan, a beautiful white shepherd, lived happily with Kavi, Prajna, and their two children. He was a big dog, but he was well behaved and easy to live with. Kavi and Prajna felt safer with Gyan around, and they felt that exercising and caring for him taught responsibility and respect for other creatures to their daughter, Ballari, and son, Naresh.

There only was one behavior that Gyan exhibited that drove them crazy: He was a beggar. It wasn't possible to eat a meal without Gyan constantly poking his nose over the edge of the table or prodding someone's knee with a paw. When friends came over for dinner, Gyan had to be locked in the basement while they ate, which only caused him to howl mournfully in frustration.

Of course, the family knew that they had caused Gyan's bad manners by feeding him tidbits from the table when he was a puppy. It had been cute when he was small, but now that he was so large, it was annoying, and they had no idea how to stop it.

I talked with Gyan and found that, in general, he was a very dignified dog. He felt that his name fit him well (Gyan means "knowledge" in Hindi), and that he was an important member of the family. I used this self-image to help us change Gyan's mind about begging. I explained that he was such a well-mannered dog that it was unbecoming for him to beg for food—it was puppy behavior, and now that he was an adult, he was expected to act like one. When put like this, he agreed.

To reinforce this request, Kavi and Prajna began teaching Gyan to stay out of the kitchen and dining areas while the family was eating, and he was fed after the family finished. He could sit or lay at the edge of the room quietly, but he was not permitted to whine or bark. If he forgot and came to the table, he was returned quietly to his place and told to sit and stay. This teaching took some repetition, because the begging habit had been reinforced for so long, but Gyan eventually got the message: The family eats first, and well-mannered dogs quietly wait their turn.

Note that Gyan did not take this personally nor did it seem strange to him. Although he had a good self-image, he also knew that he was not the leader of the pack, and this is exactly how a canine pack works: The leader and upper hierarchy eat first.

—From Danika's Casebook

Although we can't cover every behavior issue here, I think it's clear that just about any problem can be solved with patience and understanding. By using all the tools at your disposal—telepathic communication, knowledge of how the canine mind works, and training techniques—you and your dog can work together to maintain a happy, loving relationship.

It's a
Dog's Life

*"I don't like being left alone all the time. I know
Jeff hates his job and wants to go back to his old
home, where the snow is. I came from there, too,
and I want to go with him and be on the snow
hills with him and help him look out for people.
I've been waiting for him to go back there."*

—Nalla, Lab/Australian Blue heeler

Dogs, as pack animals, have a natural instinct to be members of a team. In their minds, each pack member has a job to do, and they are much more comfortable knowing that they have a useful place in the pack—it makes them feel secure.

As I've mentioned briefly in previous chapters, many dogs today find themselves in a very uncomfortable spot—they've got no job to do, and they very often have little or no mental stimulation for most of each day. They're stuck in a perpetual waiting game—hours of waiting for a few minutes of activity and attention. It's no wonder that a large percentage of the consultations I do are somehow connected to behavior problems brought on by boredom and frustration. But it doesn't have to be this way.

Doggie Daycare and Beyond

Today's lifestyle has picked up to lightning speed for many of us—gone are the days of my childhood, when sitting under a tree watching a colony of ants was enough to keep me occupied for hours. On top of long workdays and keeping up with household chores, many of us have hectic schedules of carting children to an amazing array of after-school and weekend activities. There's hardly time to eat, let alone walk the dog.

Some folks have begun to "outsource" many of the more mundane chores, such as lawn care and housecleaning. Sometimes dog care falls into this category, and I think this new trend, like anything else, has its good points and its bad points.

On the bad side, it may indicate a lifestyle that doesn't really fit with the requirements of responsible dog ownership and may demonstrate an attitude that a pet is just another "toy" to be taken care of, like a fancy car or boat—well-maintained but only played with occasionally. A dog is a social animal, and if you don't have time to socialize with one, then it's better not to invite one into your home.

On the good side, however, I think it's also an indicator that many people love their dogs very much and realize that sitting at home alone all day is not much fun for them. Doggie daycare is a booming business in the United States: thousands of dogs now enjoy regular group playtime in a safe atmosphere every day. And anyone who starts a pet-sitting business quickly finds that there are plenty of people looking for a reliable person to walk their dogs while they're at work. According to Packaged Facts, a marketing research firm that has followed the pet industry for twenty years, the pet services market is the fastest-growing pet market of all—expected to top $22 billion in 2008.

I think this expansion of services is good news for dogs and their people. It means that there's now a broad range of possibilities to choose from when you're looking for the best way to make you and your dog happy. Finding things for your dog to do is easier than ever. And when you want to do something with your dog, there are many new options, from playing at a local dog park to taking unique and fun-filled "doggie" vacations. I'd like to explore some of them with you in this chapter.

JOBS FOR DOGS

Giving your dog a job to do isn't as difficult as you might think. Dog behavior expert Cesar Millan often helps owners redirect their dogs' unwanted behavior by providing a simple job for them to do, such as carrying water bottles in a backpack on the daily walk. This seemingly minor change does wonders for a dog's self-image—it's amazing to see how it alters the way the dog stands, holds his head, and walks on a leash. Dogs love to feel useful, just as we do.

Finding the right activity to fit your dog's purpose doesn't have to be a difficult and time-consuming process. Now that you've learned to communicate telepathically, start by simply asking. There may be something that particularly interests your dog. Just like Nalla, who wanted to do ski rescue, and Tyler, from Chapter 3, who wanted to do agility courses, your dog may have seen an activity that looked fun or interesting or that called to him in some way. A simple conversation may save you a lot of time and frustration.

If your dog doesn't give you any specifics, start by giving him a particular chore. Begin by adding small tasks to your dog's daily routine, such as making it a point to ask him to guard the house while you're away, or teaching him to bring in the newspaper or mail. If you like to garden, think about asking for help from your four-legged friend—remember Dexter from Chapter 7! Likewise, if rollerblading is your passion, let your dog pull you, if appropriate—this is great exercise for active dogs, and pulling your weight is no problem for breeds such as pit bulls, huskies, rottweilers, and other working breeds. Smaller dogs might do well as biking companions, sitting in a special safety seat or basket. (I've even seen motorcycle dogs!)

Mark This Spot!

There are many groups that provide information and programs for dogs looking for jobs to do. There's even a TV show called "Dogs with Jobs," and its Web site is an excellent source for links to these groups. Go to **www.DogsWithJobs.com**, and go to the links page.

Dogs can carry other things than water bottles as well. For instance, if you enjoy hiking together, have him carry his own water and food, as well as any other items you need for the trip that he can carry comfortably. Of course, you don't want to overload your friend, but it's surprising how much weight certain breeds can carry easily and how willingly they'll do it if they're asked.

The idea is to have fun and to provide a small job to give your dog a feeling of usefulness. As you work with your friend to teach new skills, ask her to perform each task for you, explaining what a big help it is to you. If you've already established your position as pack leader, it becomes a great motivator, because every dog wants to please the "alpha dog."

Finding the Right Job

Some breeds are more suited to certain activities, but don't assume that you automatically know what's best. Be a good sport, and check into whatever appeals to your dog before dismissing it as "impossible." For example, there have been tiny Chinese crested dogs who have done amazingly well at weight-pull contests! (This is possible because weight pull is based on the dog's weight as well as the amount pulled; e.g., if a 10-lb. dog pulls ten times his body weight, a 120-lb. dog will have to pull 1,250 lbs. to beat it.) Anyone who has owned a small dog knows that they often think they are bigger and better than any other dog, and some sports give them the chance to go head-to-head and prove it.

All kinds of activities can give purpose to your dog's life. Some dogs are happier doing physical work, while others would prefer more sedate occupations. If you have a herding dog, there are places where you can "rent" sheep for herding practice for an hour or two each week. If your pup loves the water, there are water rescue classes and diving competitions. If you have a real "people" dog, perhaps visiting hospitals or nursing homes as a therapy dog would appeal to him. There are friendly races, Frisbee competitions, and agility courses for dogs who love to run, and obedience trials and drill team and scent discrimination training for dogs who thrive on a disciplined regimen.

Mark This Spot!

If you're looking for something to give your dog's life more meaning, or just want to have a really fun doggie vacation, be sure to check out the Dog Scouts of America (DSA) Web site at **www.dogscouts.com**. This nonprofit organization was started in 1995 by Lonnie Olson, a trainer who advocates a nonviolent behavioral approach and a past president of the National Association of Dog Obedience Instructors (NADOI). She also is a member of the Association of Pet Dog Trainers (APDT), and her life ambition is to experience as many dog sports and skills as possible with her dogs.

The DSA Web site is brimming with information about an amazing assortment of fun sports and activities for dogs—from agility, backpacking, and flyball to scent discrimination, water rescue, and weight pull. The group holds week-long dog camps in Michigan, as well as three-day minicamps at locations around the country.

Just like Scouts for kids, Dog Scouts have merit badges, a handbook, and local troops. There's even a motto for the dogs: "Let us learn all that we can, so that we may become more helpful." And one for the owners: "Our dogs' lives are much shorter than our own—let's help them enjoy their time with us as much as we can."

Lonnie Olson decided to design a camp program that was more than the typical obedience training courses and focused on activities that were fun for the dogs as well as for their people. All dogs and owners are encouraged to try every activity—according to the Web site information, Lonnie's Welsh corgi, Weasel, loves sled racing and weight pull. One of the newest additions to the classes is painting—the Web site even shows admirable examples of art created by the dogs. Everything is done with the dogs in mind, and all the skills are taught through encouragement and nonpunishment-based training methods to "improve the quality of their lives and make them a more valuable resource to the community."

You'll be sure to find something at Dog Scouts of America that you and your dog can enjoy together.

Your dog might love backpacking, skiing, or camping, just like you. Or maybe relaxing in a canoe, lying on the beach, or wandering behind you in the garden, pulling a cart, would suit him better. The idea here is that there is a nearly unlimited assortment of activities and jobs for dogs, and if you take the time to look, you can find to something to suit both of you.

Vacation Time

When I say "dog-friendly vacations," some of you may think, "Great. Dog vacation. I hate camping." But camping with your dog, while lots of fun and exciting for the dog, is *not* the only canine-friendly vacation you can take.

There are now entire hotel and motel chains that accept pets, as well as thousands of smaller, family-owned establishments through-out the world that will happily welcome you and your dog. Some even provide onsite kennels or daycare in case you participate in a noncanine activity. It's true that some may have restrictions on size and breed, but compared to twenty-five years ago, the number of accommodations available to people traveling with their dogs truly is astounding. It's really no longer necessary to spend the money on boarding costs every time you go away (and then deal with the guilt and anxiety caused by leaving your friend behind).

Surveys have confirmed that a large majority of dog owners consider their dogs to be family members who enjoy going on vaca-tions, and many would take their dogs with them more frequently if they knew more hotels that accepted pets. And now anyone with access to the Internet can find an abundance of exciting, dog-friendly accommodations and destinations.

For example, do you like outdoor activities? How about a summertime canoe trip on a pristine lake in Ontario or hiking through the hills and valleys along the Appalachian trail in Georgia? For you winter babies, there's snowshoeing, cross-country skiing, and dog sledding trips in the Rockies. Prefer a more sedate vacation enjoying historical sites? Try any number of battlefields, historic scenic sites, and memorials, such as Valley Forge National Park in Pennsylvania, with its miles of paved walkways. Would you rather lie on a beach while the kids play Frisbee with the dog? You'll like North and South Carolina's long stretches of dog-friendly beaches.

Remember to tailor your activities to your dog's abilities. If your Great Dane spends most of his time on the couch, don't expect him to suddenly go hiking for an entire day. Likewise, if your darling Pomeranian hates to get his feet wet, he probably won't love the beach as much as you do; however, if you have a Chesapeake Bay retriever, water sports might be an excellent choice.

Don't forget to ask your dog what he would enjoy. Just as with people, the answer may change each time you ask, so be sure to check in again before each vacation. Once you've decided where you're going, visualize it for your dog, describing all the delightful scenery and fun things you'll be doing together.

Mark This Spot!

There are lots of Web sites that sell canine travel and outdoor gear. Here are three to get you started: www.TailsByTheLake.com, www.CoolDogProducts.com, and www.DrsFosterSmith.com.

Before You Go

As you plan your trip, investigate the types of accommodations and activities available, and be sure that you have the right gear for your dog to participate safely. For example, if you're going boating, and your dog is not one of the water breeds that swim well, get a safety vest for him. If you'll be walking or hiking in inclement weather or on rough terrain, and you've got a pup who's more delicate or prone to catching cold, look into appropriate weather gear. In addition, some hotels and campgrounds require that your canine friend be crated any time he's left alone—there are now handy, pop-up camping crates that pack easily.

Remember to check with your veterinarian before you go. Your dog's vaccinations should be up to date, and you may need documentation of them and of licensing in some places. Ask about preventive measures for possible parasites at your destination, such as ticks, heartworm, and fleas. A remedy for motion sickness and diarrhea also may be on your list. (Taking a supply of water from home may prevent the latter.) Your vet may be able to give you some cautionary information on any dangers specific to your destination, such as insects, wildlife, or plants. It's also a good idea to get the name and number of a vet near your destination in case of emergency.

One more thing: Please be a responsible pet owner! Keep your dog under control at all times, and be considerate of others. If you haven't already done so, take a basic obedience class before embarking on your trip. Don't leave your friend tied up at a campsite or loose in a hotel room; clean up all waste immediately, and dispose of it properly; and don't allow your dog to engage in aggressive or annoying behavior. Remember that not everyone is a dog lover. Make sure that you and your dog never give anyone an excuse to stop allowing pets at their establishment.

Mark This Spot!

If you and your family enjoy camping, check out Four Paws Kingdom (www.4pawskingdom.com) in Rutherfordton, North Carolina, a short drive from Asheville. European-born owners Meik and Birgit Bartoschek have spent the past several years transforming a 32-acre site into a dog (and dog lovers') heaven. Both husband and wife have backgrounds in the hospitality industry, and Birgit also is a well-known artist and certified agility trainer. They bill Four Paws Kingdom as "America's first and only dog-dedicated campground... committed to people who like to travel, hike, play, and have a good time with their dogs and pets."

After moving to the United States and traveling extensively with their dogs, they decided to open their own campground aimed specifically at the more than two million people who camp with their pets. Their idea of "dog-friendly accommodations" means more than just providing a walking area and boarding kennels. At Four Paws, there are plenty of things for the dogs to do: There's a fenced dog park and swimming hole, a championship-size agility course, an obedience training arena, 20 acres of natural hiking trails, and even a fenced playground specifically for small dogs.

There's a bathhouse just for the four-legged guests and an outdoor grooming station, too—so everyone can look spiffy for those yummy cookouts! Summertime events include an Easter Bone Hunt, Dog Olympics, Rally-O Obedience fun, and regular classes and workshops.

The Bartoscheks also have set up a nonprofit foundation, the Four Paws Kingdom Foundation, with the stated mission of promoting and fostering safe and responsible dog ownership through education and creation of public awareness. Their goal is "to reduce the number of abandoned and neglected dogs by providing essential expertise, knowledge and information." They strive to recreate and stabilize the human–canine bond.

The Foundation sponsors regular workshops and seminars on such topics as general dog handling, first aid, dog socialization, and behavior modification. They invite veterinarians, trainers, and others with specialized skills to conduct demonstrations and lectures on their topic of expertise. I've even done an annual communication workshop for them. They also provide fun outings for dogs from local shelters and kids from local schools.

The campground has more than forty semiwooded campsites with electric, water, and sewer hookups that accommodate everything from a tent to large class-A RVs with slideouts. There's a laundry, a modern bathhouse, free high-speed Internet, a swimming and fishing pond, a pavilion, and a camp store. They have two rental cabins as well. Rates are listed on the Web site.

Making the Trip

When pets go along on vacation, travel by motor vehicle is most common, whether it's the family car or a recreational vehicle. For some dogs, carsickness is an issue. If this is the case for your canine, it's best to deal with it *before* vacation. There are ways to eliminate some or all of the discomfort, but they require some pre-trip planning.

If your dog only gets in the car to go to the veterinarian, fear may be a major cause of the carsickness. Try slowly desensitizing your pup by taking him or her for short trips in the car over a period of days or weeks, gradually making the trips longer and longer. Remember to reassure your friend telepathically that you are not heading for a vet appointment and that adjusting to car travel will result in a happy ending: going on vacation with the family!

For some dogs, the jarring motion of stopping and starting is the culprit, which is often made worse if there is no restraint used to steady the dog. This easily is solved either by using a special seat harness that hooks into the seatbelts or by keeping the dog in a secured crate during travel. Dogs should never travel loose or tied in the back of a pickup truck! They easily could jump or be thrown from the bed or possibly hang themselves. If you cannot have the dog inside the cab, then use a proper travel crate secured to the bed of the truck.

For safety's sake, all dogs should have some method of safety restraint while traveling in a car. Otherwise, in an accident, he will be thrown about or from the vehicle. A friend of mine lost her beloved Sheltie because he was lying on the back seat when they were hit from behind—he flew forward and snapped his neck on the front seat. Many people have also lost their unrestrained dog at rest stops when someone opened the door, and the dog unexpectedly leaped out. Save yourself this agony and properly protect your friend, just as you would your children.

Another dangerous habit is letting your dog stick his head out the window while the car is moving. Not only does it invite ear, eye, and respiratory damage, but if your dog's head fits out the window, it's possible the rest of his body can go, too—especially if something particularly inviting or antagonizing happens to catch his attention. This is another example of something that you wouldn't let your child do, so don't let your dog do it, either.

Mark This Spot!

Before you travel anywhere with your dog, check out the following Web sites for some excellent tips.

- Coyote Communications (**www.coyotecommunications.com/dog camp.html**) has an extensive section of information about preparing for a trip with your dog. It provides general information and specific ideas and suggestions from seasoned travelers. For example, you'll find what to put in a canine first-aid kit and learn about the best ways to make sure your dog is easily identified if he gets lost while you're on vacation.
- At Kind Planet (**www.KindPlanet.org/travel.html**), you'll find lots of information, as well as handy checklists to print out for trip planning and pet-sitter instructions for those times when the pooch can't go.

Pawprint

IMPORTANT! *Never* leave your dog unattended in the car! On a 78°day, the temperature in a car parked in the sun reaches 160° in a matter of minutes. Even with the windows cracked or when parked in the shade, the interior temperature quickly rises beyond a dog's ability to cool himself and can result in irreparable brain damage or death by heatstroke. There also is the growing danger of kidnapping by dog fighting rings and those who provide animals to research labs. Be smart—if you wouldn't leave your child, don't leave your dog!

Flying High

Fortunately, there also are some new options for pets traveling by air. I personally would never put an animal friend in a crate destined for the cargo hold of an airliner——there have been too many instances of death due to freezing, heatstroke, stress, and untended medical conditions. Not only are these areas not pressurized, heated, or air-conditioned, but the animals are subjected to extreme noise levels, rough handling, and other traumatizing horrors. Pets are not baggage!

Happily, small dogs are now finding a safe haven in the passenger cabin of more commercial flights, and I have heard of larger dogs occupying a passenger seat, at the cost of an additional ticket, of course. There are some new, smaller companies that cater specifically to people traveling with their pets and that permit the animals to fly onboard the planes.

Chartering a small plane is another option, and this may be less expensive than you think. Check with your local small-craft airport. Some pilots will fly you and your pet for little more than the cost of fuel if they happen to be going to the same destination as you. On privately owned planes, it's up to the owner whether dogs are allowed and whether they must be crated. Also, many small planes fly at lower altitudes that do not require pressurization, which eliminates another potential discomfort for your pet.

If you're flying, please remember to prepare your friend well ahead of time by having a number of conversations honestly describing what to expect—the loud noise, the pressure changes, etc.—and listen to your dog's concerns. It may be worthwhile to take your dog on a trip to your local airport to get a first-hand view of what you've described. If your dog is adamant about not flying, respect that and look into other modes of transportation, if possible.

Whether you're driving or flying, be sure that your dog is comfortable in the travel crate, if one is required. If you don't already have a crate, plan ahead and acquire one well before your trip so that your dog can get used to it. If possible, put the sleeping cushion or bed that's used at home into the crate to give an added feeling of security. (You also can try putting a towel over the home bed and allowing the dog to sleep on it for a few days before leaving, then putting the newly scented towel in the crate.)

If you think it might be necessary, talk to your veterinarian about mild sedation for the trip. However, it's important to note that if you are flying, sedation can cause respiratory and/or cardiovascular problems at increased altitudes. The Bach flower essence called "Rescue Remedy" is helpful in calming anxious pets as well—you can spray it in the crate before leaving and add a squirt or two during the trip, if necessary. You can purchase Bach flower essences at many health food stores or online.

The RV Experience

Another option for vacation is renting a recreational vehicle, or RV, either from a large company such as Cruise America or from private RV owners. You also may be able to rent a camping trailer or cabin at some campgrounds. There are many styles to choose from, and depending on size, most sleep four to eight people comfortably, so you can find the one that fits your family best.

Although it's similar to camping, RVing is a whole lot more comfortable. Today, most rental RVs have microwaves, coffeemakers, air-conditioning and heating, large refrigerators/freezers, stoves, TVs, and their own full bathrooms, as well as stylish and comfortable furniture. Some even have master bedrooms, a washer/dryer, a garden tub, awnings, screen rooms, and lots more!

If you're concerned about the drivability of an RV, don't be. I have owned and rented several of them, ranging in size from 23 feet to 38 feet (plus towing a car or boat), and they all handle extremely well. The class C vehicles are the most like driving a pickup truck— they're built on a truck frame and generally have one of the sleeping areas over the cab.

There are some advantages to taking an RV rather than a car. You have greater flexibility than when you stay in a hotel and, in some ways, a bit more privacy. You can go places with an RV where there are no other accommodations. Some attractions and destinations have RV parks connected to them, which eliminates the need for a daily drive and parking hassle. You also can save money on food, because you can cook your own meals instead of eating out all the time. Many RV parks have activities to keep the whole family happy, and in my experience, RVing folks are a very friendly bunch. The RV also provides a safe environment for your dog in case you have to leave him or her behind for part of the day, although if you plan to be away for a long period, you probably should check into doggie daycare or boarding.

Mark This Spot!

There are plenty of Web sites to help you plan your vacation. I have a Web site dedicated to traveling with your dog, with regular updates of new pet-friendly locations tested by actual dog owners, at www.HappyDogTravel.com. There also are two sites that provide directories and reservation services for hotels that advertise as pet-friendly accommodations: www.BringYourPet.com/index.htm and www.PetsWelcome.com. Companion air is a new airline that caters to pet owners (www.CompanionAir.com). If you are considering renting an RV, try www.GoRVing.com or www.CruiseAmerica.com, which are large commercial organizations, or www.MotorHomeRental.ws, which has a directory of privately owned RVs for rent.

These are just a few examples of the endless possibilities that are now available to you and your dog on your next vacation together. Try your own online search for pet-friendly accommodations, destinations, and activities. You'll find guide books, tour operators, and directories with enough information and suggestions for a lifetime of fun!

In the next chapter, we'll talk about your pet's health and how using your new communication skills can help keep your dog comfortable and healthy.

Your Dog's Health

"Skye always has been such an active, happy Border collie. Whenever the kids are in the backyard, you're sure to see a tri-color blur as she races around with them. So when she began moping around one morning, not even interested in going outside, I knew something was up. After calling to make a vet appointment, I sat down to chat with her telepathically. As soon as I tuned in to Skye, I got a horrible headache and felt dizzy and sick to my stomach. When I asked her if she knew what was wrong, she told me she had been chasing a squirrel and ran full speed into the leg of the swing set. No one had seen this happen, but when we went to the vet, I asked her to check for a concussion, and sure enough, that's what they found."

—Amanda W.

Whenever a loved one is not feeling well, we feel their pain and want to relieve it—this is a natural extension of the close bond we form with those around us. However, our human family members, with the exception of infants, usually are able to tell us where it hurts or what is wrong. Unfortunately, our canine companions don't have the same ability to speak to the vet or point to the area of their pain. This is where your telepathic communication skills come in.

When you live with a dog, you learn what's "normal" behavior for that particular dog. For example, some breeds are laze-abouts, and you expect them to doze for hours and hours each day, while such extended sleeping in another breed is cause for concern. Likewise, your pup may be a voracious eater with a high metabolism who wants to munch all the time, while your neighbor's pet may eat only out of necessity; both may be considered normal. Getting to know your dog's regular habits is an important part of being a good pet owner, and it's a lifelong job, because as your puppy grows, some habits will change.

For example, a young puppy may need to relieve himself every hour or two throughout the day, but an adult dog may be fine with three or four trips outside. If your young puppy suddenly stops urinating or your adult dog suddenly requires numerous trips, you would notice the change immediately and should see your veterinarian.

When you notice a change in your dog's normal behavior, use your telepathic communications skills to help your dog tell you what's wrong. Sometimes, it's just a case of the "blahs" or a bid for attention. This often happens when there's a change in the household, such as a new infant arriving or someone moving out. At other times, the information you receive will tell you that you have an urgent situation brewing that, if handled quickly, can be avoided or at least diminished in severity.

CALL THE VET FIRST!

It is imperative to note that telepathic communication should never, I repeat, *never* be used instead of seeking veterinary help! If you have a medical situation of any kind, take your dog to the veterinarian *first,* and then talk with your animal either at the vet's office, if you feel comfortable doing so, or after you come home. If your child had an urgent medical problem, you would go directly to the doctor or hospital and then ask specifics later—do the same for your furry family member.

Pawprint

Always consult a veterinarian first for any medical problems your dog may have. Animal communication never is a substitute for proper medical care!

I'm sure that you notice almost immediately when something's wrong with your dog, but knowing *what* is wrong can be a little trickier. If you've maintained a good level of communication with your pal throughout his life, you will find it much easier to get information about illnesses when they occur. Although it's possible to have your first telepathic conversation with your dog when you're trying to determine a medical issue, I don't recommend it—due to the stress on both of you, you probably will have better luck working with a professional animal communicator or someone who is more emotionally detached.

Doggie Diaries

Over the years, I have done many consultations for people whose pets have some medical condition. My first question always is, "Have you seen a vet for this problem?" I am not a doctor and therefore am not qualified to give medical advice. However, part of my gift is to be able to discern hidden physical or emotional issues. It is not something I learned with animal communication; it is something that just happens, sometimes without my conscious intent. Once I began developing and practicing my telepathic abilities, however, I was able to dig a little deeper and get better information.

One case in particular stands out in my memory. I was participating in a spiritual healing circle, and a woman whom I had seen once or twice at the group began telling about a female Lhasa apso that had been rushed to the vet the day before. She started by saying that her friend's dog had been in the backyard and suddenly yelped in pain. She and her friend ran outside and found the dog near a small hole in the ground. Thinking the dog had stumbled and broken or fractured her leg, they immediately took her to the vet for treatment.

The vet could find no broken bones and no fractures, sprains, or anything else wrong, but the pup began to deteriorate quickly, her hind legs going lame and then becoming paralyzed. The vet was mystified, and so was the woman and her friend.

As I listened to this story, I had a sudden, sharp, stabbing pain in my abdomen, and the words, "That dog was poisoned!" sprang loudly from my mouth. Believe me, I was more shocked than anyone in the room at my sudden outburst, as all faces turned to stare in my direction. I had not been communicating consciously with the dog, although it is possible that she urgently needed to give the information, and I simply was attuned to receiving it.

The end result is that the woman told her friend to call the vet and have blood work done. The vet found that the dog had indeed eaten rat poison, and she then was given treatment to counteract it. The little Lhasa took some time to recover from the incident, but she eventually regained full use of her legs.

Other similar instances have led me to conclude that there are times when the situation is so urgent that I am merely a channel for information, from either the pet or the Universe, for a reason of which I'm not aware.

—*From Danika's Casebook*

ANATOMY 101

Before you attempt to confer about medical issues with your dog, I suggest that you become familiar with basic canine anatomy. Although humans and canines both are mammals, it's obvious that there are some physical differences. Knowing the similarities and distinctions will make it much easier to translate correctly information you receive.

It's easy enough to go on the Internet or to the library and find illustrations of various canine body parts and internal organs. You even may find a handy chart that you can use for reference during communications with your dog. Seeing all the elements and having the correct names only can help you locate and define a problem with more precision.

For instance, did you know that dogs don't walk on their "feet"? Instead, they walk on four toes. Their ankles (on their back legs) and wrists (on their front legs) do not touch the ground when they walk. These joints actually sit just above their dewclaw, which is a vestigial fifth toe. Some people mistakenly believe these joints to be the dog's knees and elbows and wonder why they bend "backward."

Once you've taken a crash course in canine anatomy, find yourself a quiet spot and prepare to communicate with your dog. You don't have to wait until there's an obvious problem. In fact, you may be able to prevent some illnesses by catching symptoms very early through regular checks of your dog's body.

EXERCISE 9

Scanning

When I check for medical issues, I generally start by doing a mental scan of the animal's body. Physical sensations, visual images, or feelings occur in my own body, and I translate their location and meaning to the proper location on the dog's body. Only after completing the scan do I have a conversation with the dog about what I've found. There are several reasons for this: It clarifies the information for me in case the dog is unable to clearly identify the problem, and it gives me something to work with if the dog is avoiding an issue.

Here's how to scan your own pet to check for medical problems:

1.   Settle yourself, close your eyes, and take a moment to scan your own body and emotional state. Note any problems or symptoms you may have so that you don't confuse them with your dog's. If you are ill yourself or have a physical ailment that interferes with your ability to telepathically communicate, try again later when you're feeling better. Or, if the situation is of a more urgent nature, ask a friend or a professional animal communicator for help. For instance, I know that if I have a bad headache before I start, I will not receive good information, so I'll refer a client to another communicator if the consultation can't wait.

2.   Now that you are aware of your own physical and mental state, close your eyes again and begin to focus your attention on your dog's body. Mentally scan each body part, starting with the head and working gradually to the tail. Take your time with each one, noting any physical sensations or emotions that arise in your own body. Remember to translate the location of any physical sensations to the proper spot on your dog's body. (This is where the

canine anatomy lesson comes in handy!)

3. Be as specific as possible, moving on to the next body part only when you stop receiving information. You may feel an ache in your neck, for instance. Is it dull or sharp? Does moving your head make it worse or better? Do you have a sudden feeling of fear or anxiety? Make note of whatever information you receive, either by writing it down, having someone else take notes, or speaking into a recorder.

4. It's possible that you'll receive auditory signals, visual images, or even scents when you are performing your scan. Make a note of these as well, without judging their content. What may seem ridiculous at first glance may be a unique way of identifying a problem. For example, I once did a scan of a dog in serious pain and received an image of what I took to be Swiss cheese. When connected with other information I gathered, it became clear that this was a graphic illustration of bone cancer, which was indeed what the dog was suffering from.

5. Don't be concerned if the information isn't completely clear at first. As with the "Swiss cheese" example, there are times when what you receive isn't translated easily. At other times, the problem may stem from an emotional issue that has long been suppressed and has been triggered by a recent event. It's also possible that your dog simply doesn't want to share the information with you, which you may find out when you converse directly with him or her. We will address this in a minute.

6. When you've completed your scan, review the information, and look for clues and connections that may give you an indication of a problem. For example, several areas of dull aching in joints could signal arthritis. Cloudiness of vision could indicate the beginnings of cataracts. Again, remember that you are not diagnosing anything —simply gathering information that may be helpful in suggesting a cause or path of action.

7. Next, use your regular techniques for telepathically communicating with your dog. Have a conversation about his general health: How are you feeling today? Does anything hurt? Why are you limping (or coughing or sluggish)? Allow your pet to answer you—don't

jump in with what you think you already know. When you receive an answer to a question, you may want to clarify with a statement such as, "When I scanned you just now, I felt a stiffness in your shoulder area. Are you sore there?" or whatever is relevant to the situation.

8. It's possible that your dog may not wish to speak with you about health issues. Just as your children sometimes will gloss over a problem because they don't want to go to the doctor, a pet also may try to avoid a trip to the vet's. In this case, you may get better information from another pet in the household or from another animal communicator—there often is a four-legged "tattler" in the house, or perhaps your pet will open up to an outsider more readily.

9. Once you've completed the scan and the conversation, you should have some useful information to guide you in choosing the next step. If you're just checking in to see how your dog is doing, you may want to jot down the information in a journal with the date so that you have an ongoing record of your dog's day-to-day health. If you are addressing a specific problem, you may want to share the information with your vet. If you uncover an emotional issue, you can look for ways to alleviate the situation that's causing it. (See page 156 for more on emotional issues.)

10. If you get information that is confusing or that you are unable to translate into something recognizable, you may want to seek validation from a friend or professional communicator. When dealing with your own pets, it is especially easy to misread or misinterpret due to your own assumptions or fears. Never be afraid to get a second opinion.

11. A special note about working with your veterinarian: Be aware that not all vets believe in animal communication, and some even are antagonistic toward any information about symptoms obtained this way. If this sounds like your vet, you may want to provide the information in a way that seems more "normal"—that is, without reference to your telepathic conversation. Although you might think veterinarians are prime candidates for using the technique,

the reality is that much of their scientific training tells them that it's just not possible. However, some do recognize its value, and others, by virtue of their training in holistic animal care, are more likely to appreciate its use.

Doggie Diaries

I once did a consultation for Theresa, whose female Akita, Julep, had been having digestive problems. Over a period of several weeks, the dog had been continually vomiting after eating, although she seemed otherwise healthy. Their veterinarian had checked for many illnesses and diseases, had done blood work and x-rays, and could discover nothing wrong. Finally, he suggested trying several different foods, thinking that perhaps Julep was allergic to certain ingredients. Nothing helped, and the dog continued to vomit and began to lose weight rapidly. By the time Theresa contacted me, she was completely distraught over Julep's deteriorating condition and frustrated by her inability to help her beloved dog.

When I did a scan of Julep's body, I could sense an obstruction somewhere high in my large intestine, something thin and triangular, and of a material that might not readily appear on an x-ray. In my conversation with Julep, I kept hearing the word "koosh," which didn't make much sense to me. I asked Theresa if she and Julep played with a "koosh ball"—a squishy rubber toy with tiny rubber strands all over—but she said no. That was all the information that I was able to get from Julep—just that there definitely was an obstruction and the word "koosh" over and over.

Theresa was determined to save Julep, and she went back to the vet and insisted that he do an exploratory surgery as a last resort. He finally agreed, since nothing else had seemed to help. During the surgery, the veterinarian pulled a 3- to 4-inch triangular piece of a padded shoe insole out of Julep's large intestine. He was amazed and apologetic, and he did not even charge Theresa for the surgery.

Later, I received a call from Theresa, ecstatically telling me the results of the surgery. She said, "When the doctor told me what he'd found, I remembered you getting the word 'koosh' from Julep. I think she was trying to say 'cushion,' which is just what the insole looked like before she ate it!"

—From Danika's Casebook

DEALING WITH EMOTIONAL ISSUES

The emotional bonds we create with our dogs are as strong and lifelong as those with other family members. Indeed, they feel the same way toward us. It is not surprising, then, to see how changes in family situations can affect dogs emotionally and, as with humans, how these emotions can cause physical problems if left unaddressed.

A common example is the dog who becomes jealous when a new baby joins the family. Once the king of the roost and sole center of attention, the pooch now must adjust to being second banana. For many dogs, especially those who have been accustomed to being the alpha, this is a serious problem. It is not unlike the firstborn child reacting resentfully when the new sibling demands more of her parents' attention. Unfortunately, due to the pack mentality of the canine psyche, this situation tends to cause aggressive behaviors, and too often, the dog's natural tendencies result in the loss of his place in the family and perhaps even his life.

This is one case in particular when developing your position as a loving, dominant pack leader from the start of your relationship will avoid painful consequences later. Every human in the house must be seen as a pack leader: if your dog does not see all housemembers that way, she will feel an innate need to challenge their positions. Of course, this trait may be more prevalent in some dogs than in others. Although it is not as gender-specific as some people think—many female dogs are "alphas"; you know your own dog best.

Other emotional upheavals can cause turmoil in your dog's life as well. For instance, if you and your spouse raised your dog together and at some point you decide to divorce, there will be a period of distress over the loss of whichever "parent" leaves. There also may be conflicted feelings during the period after a decision is made to split up but before anyone actually moves out.

I once did a consultation with a woman who knew that her mixed-breed dog, Jericho, was very upset over the impending breakup of her marriage. Jericho didn't know where to place his loyalty, because he loved the husband and the wife equally. He felt that he should stay with the woman as her protector, even though he still wanted to take part in the activities he enjoyed with the man. Jericho was confused and depressed. Happily, it was an amicable divorce, and after the consultation, both parties agreed to continue participating in Jericho's life as much as possible.

Likewise, if your dog was raised with your child, expect some separation anxiety to crop up when college time arrives. If a family member dies, remember that your dog certainly will most grieve with the rest of the family. I have seen pets who are so distraught over the loss of their lifelong companions that they sit in a dark closet all day, or refuse to eat, or develop destructive behaviors to take out their frustrations or gain attention. Obviously, when your dog is in emotional pain, you must do whatever you can to help. Just being aware of what's causing the difficulty is a big first step toward a solution.

By doing a scan of your pet's body and asking questions about his feelings, you often can ascertain the underlying issues that may be causing physical ailments. Treating emotional problems requires sensitivity to your dog's normal mental state and an understanding of the typical canine psychological makeup.

In the end, your willingness to listen and respond with compassion probably is the biggest help when it comes to troubles concerning emotions. Although you may not be able to take away the pain completely, your efforts at working through the situation with your dog will make a difference and ultimately will result in a stronger bond and a happier life for you both.

Rescued Dogs and Emotional Baggage

If you have adopted a rescued dog, you are an extraordinary person who has opened your heart to a dog with special needs. Some dogs from rescues and shelters have a history of abuse and neglect, although a large percentage of animals have been surrendered for other reasons, such as family relocation; divorce, death, or illness of an owner; or poor understanding of what dog ownership requires.

Whatever the reason, any dog separated from his family will bear emotional scars from the experience. Often there has been no effort to communicate the circumstances to the dog, leaving large gaps in information that bewilders and upsets the pup. Like human children who assume that they are the cause of their parents' divorce, dogs will often erroneously "fill in the blanks" and take on guilt for their rejection, even though it isn't justified.

This is a prime opportunity for you to use your telepathic skills to help you and your friend deal with the baggage of the past and create a better future together. You may have had conversations with your canine companion in the process of selecting him from the rescue or shelter, and that is a good start. As you live together and get to know each other, what you learn telepathically will add to the overall picture of your dog's mental and physical health.

Note that an event may trigger an unexpected emotional or physical response, and it may be a catalyst to further conversations that delve deeper into your dog's past. For example, simply jingling your keys might cause one dog to happily anticipate a car ride, while another with a shadowed past might recognize it as a signal for banishment to an outdoor cage. If at all possible, take time when the event occurs to address the situation and its cause: It will be fresh in your dog's mind, and you will have a better chance at changing the association to something more positive.

Don't be surprised if at first your friend is unwilling to discuss the past. Be sensitive to the pain he may have suffered, and be gentle with your approach. Holding frequent short conversations may be more productive than a long session "on the couch," so to speak. Make it clear that you accept and love him regardless of the past, and that you are ready to help whenever it is desired. Take it one step at a time, and treat each problem that arises as a separate issue.

Some dogs have spent years in tremendous psychological pain, and it may take years to work through it all and get past it. Keep reminding yourself as you go that your love and patience are the best medicines to heal wounds like these, and that your dog deserves a happy, healthy, and loving home.

A WORD ABOUT EUTHANASIA

Sometimes, despite our best efforts, we come to a point when a very difficult decision must be made: whether we should euthanize our beloved dog. Of all the consultations that I do, the ones about euthanasia are without a doubt the most difficult. Having been in the situation myself, I know how disturbing it is to be faced with the decision to end a friend's life, no matter what the reason.

One thing I know, however, is that animals do not have the fear of death that many humans have. Although they value their lives as much as we do, dogs and other creatures have imparted to me an understanding that death is part of life, and that crossing over is not something to be feared. (Chapter 12, beginning on page 185, is devoted to the topic of saying good-bye to your dog and continuing to connect with him after death.)

When you have maintained a lifelong communication with your dog, you are as well equipped as you can be if you are faced with the possibility of choosing euthanasia. Have a conversation just as you would for any other medical or emotional issue, and find out how your pet feels and what his wishes are. Once you have the information, you will be better able to make a decision that fits those wishes.

Doggie Diaries

Alice had several Airedales over the years, and she absolutely loved the breed. However, in the past two years, she had been forced to put down a dog each year. They apparently had succumbed to a mysterious illness that struck at about four years of age and included symptoms such as convulsions, fever, and gastrointestinal distress.

Now Zephyr, her youngest, was showing the same problems, and the vet was suggesting euthanasia. Alice was totally distraught over the thought of losing yet another dog. She contacted me, because she wanted to find out what Zephyr wanted her to do.

I tuned in to the young male Airedale and felt a shivering, shaking feeling all over my body. It was not shivering from cold or fever or convulsions but from fear. When I asked Zephyr how he felt, he clearly indicated that although he was not feeling well, he was not ready to die and was sure that he would get well. He was shaking with fear because he was afraid that he would be euthanized the next day, before his body had the chance to recover.

This was extraordinary: Zephyr was the first dog who had ever expressed a fear of dying to me. Most canines and other animals I have spoken with are not afraid of death, especially when they are sick or old. I asked Zephyr to confirm the information, and he asserted again that he felt that he would get better and did not want to be euthanized.

This presented a difficult situation for me. I am not a veterinarian, and I certainly did not want to contradict a professional opinion. However, I felt bound by my duty to Zephyr to make the information known to Alice. I told her that although most dogs do not express a fear of dying, Zephyr clearly did, and he also conveyed a wish to remain alive until his body could heal.

I knew how upsetting this was for Alice, but she had asked to know what Zephyr wanted. In the end, she was the only one who could make the decision, and the information from Zephyr gave her more information to work with. Zephyr indicated that he was not in a high degree of pain, so there didn't seem to be a pressing need for quick euthanasia.

Two days after the consultation, I received a phone call from Alice. She was in tears and could hardly speak, but what she said sent a shiver down my spine. She had listened to what Zephyr shared through me, then went back to the vet and said that she wanted to wait a day or two before making a final decision, and the veterinarian agreed.

Late on the day after our call, Zephyr had begun to come around—the fever had broken, he had stopped convulsing, and he had started to eat. By the second morning, he was back to his normal self, and he was anxious to go home! Alice and the vet were amazed. She was overjoyed at the prospect of bringing her baby home and so thankful that I was able to convey Zephyr's wishes. Needless to say, the news brought tears of joy to my eyes as well!

—From Danika's Casebook

In this chapter, we've covered some basic issues and techniques for helping you deal with your dog's health. In the next, we'll talk about how dogs also can help you with yours!

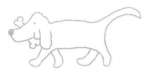

How Dogs Can Help with Your Health

"Takeo has been with me now for about two years. Since a car accident several years ago, I have had seizures regularly. I adopted Takeo from an Akita rescue, because I live alone. Little did I know that he would change my life!

A month after Takeo arrived, I started noticing that sometimes he would urgently push at my hand with his head. At first, I thought it was just to get attention. However, it soon became clear that whenever he did this, in about ten minutes I'd have a seizure. He'd had no training as an alert dog, but I learned to pay attention to his nudging and get down on the floor where I'd be safe. After a seizure, I'd always come to with Takeo on my chest, licking my face and protecting my body with his. I no longer have to worry about having a seizure in a dangerous place and hurting myself!"

—Tomasu H.

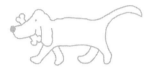

I n recent decades, the world's medical and scientific communities have generated much scholarly research that affirms what many pet owners have known all along: Living with a pet is good for you.

Respected journals, such as the *Journal of the American Medical Association (JAMA)*, *The Lancet*, *The American Journal of Cardiology*, and *Journal of the American Geriatrics Society*, among others, have published articles and the results of extensive studies that indicate how pet ownership positively influences our physical and psychological health.

Aside from the obvious benefits of increased exercise and unconditional love, pets contribute to our health in many ways. It's been shown that pet owners have lower cholesterol, stronger immune systems, and fewer minor health problems; take fewer medications; and have lowered stress levels. Elderly pet owners remain active and self-sufficient longer, and pets enhance the mental stability of those who suffer from bipolar disorder.

Studies now have been done in a wide spectrum of specialties, including how pet-assisted therapy improves rehabilitation in stroke patients, how dog owners recover more quickly from heart attacks, how a dog's touch can "unfreeze" a Parkinson's patient, and how a service dog can help socialize autistic children. It even appears that the mere presence of a pet in the home can help hypertension patients control their blood pressure, and pets help children develop stronger immune systems and have fewer allergies.

Mark This Spot!

Seattle's Swedish Medical Center has interesting articles about the benefits of owning a dog on its Web site, **www.swedish.org/15309.cfm**.

ANIMALS AS HEALERS

These studies certainly bolster the belief in animals as healers, which has been around for millennia. Indeed, many of the world's indigenous peoples have looked to the animal kingdom for healing since before the beginning of written history. Various creatures have been sought as teachers and guides, sometimes working with or through shamans or healers to effect cures or suggest treatments. Sometimes, animals have appeared as personal totems or protectors for individuals with an affinity for a particular animal.

In many cultures, animals always have been seen as equals with humans. Some cultures also have seen them as retaining abilities and senses that humans somehow have lost. Although these cultures have at times killed the sacred animals and used their bodies for food, clothing, healing, and other purposes, such killing usually has been performed ceremoniously and with great respect for the gifts animals provide. Such killing rarely if ever has been done casually or wastefully in such cultures.

My personal belief is that we have much to learn from the world's nonhuman beings, and in the end, they may hold the key to saving the planet and possibly humanity as well.

DOG DOCTORS

In my work as an animal communicator, I have done enough consultations with people whose pets have come into their lives with the specific job of healing them that I am convinced that certain animals are healers, just as certain humans are. Sundance's story below illustrates this very well.

As you can see from Sundance's story, some animals are natural healers. They seem to be born with a special gift for taking

Doggie Diaries

Sundance always was a very loving, attentive dog. She came to us when she was just eight weeks old, a lanky, playful, black-and-white English setter puppy. As she grew to her full size, she always seemed to be older and wiser than her age.

When Sundance was about four years old, my wife, Beryl, developed bone cancer. As she went through tests and chemotherapy, she often was sick and exhausted. Through it all, Sundance never left her side. She'd sit for hours with her head in Beryl's lap or snuggled against her on the couch.

Several months into this terrible situation, Sundance began to show ominous signs of deteriorating health and was diagnosed *with the same cancer as my wife*. What was even more strange was that while the progression of Beryl's cancer slowed, Sundance became sicker.

We did an animal communication consultation and found out that Sundance was a "healing dog" who was working to draw Beryl's cancer out and into herself. We'd never heard about healing dogs, but it certainly seemed that our beautiful girl was doing just that. Of course, this greatly upset Beryl—she didn't want Sundance to die because of her. However, we were told that Sundance had chosen this path and was honored to give her life for us. She felt that this was her calling and said that in a past life, she had been a healer who had misused her skills.

As time went on, Sundance continued to get sicker, and she finally passed away about a year later. Beryl lived another two years after that, and she always said that she knew her life was extended because of Sundance's healing.

—Preston R.

on another's illness. Obviously, not all dogs do this, but most dogs do have an innate ability to detect when their pack members are not feeling well or are under stress of some kind.

It often happens that when I do a consultation for someone whose dog is exhibiting odd or negative behavior, the cause is actually an upsetting situation in the owner's life. Many people do not realize how sensitive their dogs are and how easily their own behavior affects their pets'.

This may be how seizure-alert dogs can sense an oncoming seizure in their owner. Although this phenomenon is not completely understood, it's possible that the human exhibits subconscious changes in behavior just prior to a seizure—changes so subtle that only an animal used to reading minute changes in body language would notice.

Once you've lived with a dog for a while, you may notice how your mood affects your pet. If you're not feeling well, you may find that every time you sit down, you've got a furry head in your lap and a warm body snuggled up against you. Or you may notice that whenever you're in the dumps, your dog is more insistent about going for a walk or bringing you a toy for play—anything to get you out and moving.

You probably don't realize how much you reveal about yourself by minor changes in your normal behavior. Because much of the information canines gather about each other is based on body language, it's only natural that your pack member picks up on it.

Helpful Tips

Here are some ways for you to work with your dog's natural desire to help you. Keep in mind that some dogs will have more interest in this and be better at it than others. Some skills, such as sensing an oncoming seizure, are very rare. Others may require extensive training, such as those exhibited by service dogs. Don't judge your dog unkindly if it's not in his nature to participate in the way you'd like—the many other wonderful qualities of living with a canine will contribute to your good health anyway!

- When you have a regular conversation with your dog, ask if there's anything he would like to ask or share about you. Take the time to listen to your friend—you may be surprised at what you hear! Sometimes your dog will have a concern or notice that something's up even before you do. Just as human family members may notice changes and provide helpful feedback or support, so too can your canine family members. You might want to keep notes of these conversations: The information may prove helpful to you later.

- If you are facing a difficult or stressful situation, whether it's health-, relationship-, or job-related, sit quietly with your dog and talk about what's going on. Share your feelings, fears, and concerns. You be the judge of what your dog is able to handle— the idea is not to upset your pet but to enlist support.

Obviously, you wouldn't unload something traumatic on a puppy or a dog that's already anxious any more than you would on a child. However, more mature dogs often know when something is going on, and they'll appreciate being given the information and the opportunity to help. Remember that not only will you feel better for sharing your burden, but you'll be reassuring your dog that any behavior changes are due to the stress of the situation not a problem with him.

While asking for understanding during the troubling time, be sure to ask for support in a specific way (such as, "I'll need your help to carry things" or "I may need you to stay close to me"). Dogs absolutely love to have a job to do, and the work will help them get through the tough times, too.

- If you are prone to regular periods of depression or anxiety, you may want to enlist your dog's help in detecting subtle changes that lead to it. Explain your condition and your symptoms, and ask your dog to be aware of changes in your personality and suggest actions that will help pull you out of the downward slide. It may be to alert you with a particular behavior, such as a persistent nudge to your hand or knee, or by insisting on more playtime or walks—anything that triggers your mind so that you may take the steps necessary to alleviate your depression or anxiety before it takes hold of you. (For information about specially trained psychiatric service dogs, check out **www.psychdog.org.**)

- You may use this same technique for other health issues that have somewhat standard, non–life-threatening warning symptoms, such as high blood pressure, diabetes, hypoglycemia, or conditions that are triggered by elevated stress levels. For example, when a person's blood sugar level drops, there are certain behaviors that are common. A dog may notice these changes sooner and signal the person to get something to eat. Explain your specific symptoms in detail, and suggest certain actions that your dog can do to benefit you. For example, if you start to get anxious or angry, your dog could lick your face to remind you to calm down before your blood pressure rises. Or, if you start to mumble, it signifies that you need to eat, so your dog could grab a banana from a bowl and bring it to you. Remember that each dog is different; you will have to decide what is appropriate for your dog and you. If you want to train your dog to alert or assist you, there are professional organizations that do that. Check out the links page of **www.DogsWithJobs.com** for an extensive list.

- *NOTE: Be sensible! Do not rely solely on your dog to notify you of health conditions unless he is professionally trained to do so! Follow your normal healthcare regimen and seek professional help when necessary; your dog's input is extra information only.*

- When you're not feeling well, talk with your dog about your illness, explaining in as much detail as you feel appropriate. Take time to listen to what your dog has to say about the situation, answer any concerns or questions, and willingly accept whatever support your friend wishes to provide. Sometimes what you really need is just to have someone who loves you sit or lie next to you quietly, and many dogs are really great at this, especially when they know you are ill. This natural ability is partly what makes pet-assisted therapy work so well.

Mark This Spot!

Although dogs have shorter life spans than we do, it's possible for your dog to outlive you, or for you to become ill and unable to care for your friend. You can prepare for this unfortunate circumstance by leaving instructions about your wishes. The Humane Society of the United States has produced an excellent guide to help you provide for the care of your pets in the event that something happens to you. Go to their Web site at **www.hsus.org**, and type "Providing for Your Pet's Future Without You" in the search box.

Doggie Diaries

Giselle has owned Matisse since he was eight weeks old. He already was a five-year-old standard poodle when Giselle was diagnosed with a heart murmur that could cause her to black out if she got overly stressed. The condition itself caused some anxiety and, as always with important things in her life, Giselle talked to her best friend, Matisse, about it.

The elegant and intelligent dog always had been a big part of Giselle's life, but after the diagnosis, he became her constant companion. In general, poodles are very attuned to their owner's moods and feelings; Matisse seemed to be a specialist. Whenever he detected a slight rise in Giselle's anxiety level, he would gently lick her hands and face, forcing her to focus on him and distracting her from the cause of the stress.

Many times he intervened when some minor incident could have escalated Giselle's stress and caused her to black out in public. One time, a bicyclist speeding down a busy road didn't see them getting ready to cross the street and cut them off—they were not in any real danger, but it was aggravating nonetheless. Giselle started to get angry, but Matisse immediately began licking her hand to calm her down. It was just enough to distract her from the situation and to allow her to decide to let it go.

As the years, pass and as Giselle lives with her condition, she's grown to depend on Matisse to keep her grounded and calm. She knows that her companion understands her problem, and she knows to trust his guidance—he has allowed her to continue to live a normal life.

—From Danika's Casebook

PET-ASSISTED THERAPY

Also known as pet-facilitated therapy, pet-assisted therapy is the use of dogs, cats, or other pets to speed the recovery or improve the well-being of people in a wide variety of situations. The term "pet-assisted therapy" applies to such a broad field that it includes dogs employed to soothe survivors and workers at disaster sites, dogs who visit hospitals to cheer patients during long hospitalizations, dogs who actively participate in physical therapy regimens of stroke and accident victims, dogs who are trained to help autistic children to socialize or learning-disabled children to read, and dogs who help elderly Alzheimer's patients maintain mental stability and physical activity for as long as possible.

We've mentioned already dogs who sense oncoming seizures and high stress levels. There also are alert dogs for those with bipolar disorder and other emotional disabilities, dogs who are able to "sniff out" cancer tumors, and dogs who assist the blind, deaf, and those confined to wheelchairs to lead normal lives. This is just a short list of some of the many ways in which dogs are helping to heal people.

There's one a Chihuahua named Wheely Willy whose rear legs are paralyzed. He has his own specially designed wheelchair, and he travels around the world helping children with disabilities cope with their situations and see that nothing is impossible. Willy has been on national television many times, visits hospitals weekly, and even led a group of children with spinal injuries in the L.A. marathon!

Doggie Diaries

Willy was found in a cardboard box in L.A., left to die with his spinal cord crushed and his vocal chords cut. A passerby took him to a veterinarian for emergency care. Then the Chihuahua was adopted by Deborah Turner, who recognized a special spark in him. Deborah took him home and got him a specially designed wheelchair.

Far from being a pitiful little dog, "Wheely Willy" is full of joy and life, and he and Deborah travel around the world bringing a message of hope and determination everywhere they go. They regularly visit hospital wards, work with disabled kids, and make special appearances. Learn more about this remarkable little Chihuahua with the "can-do" attitude at **www.wheelywilly.com**.

—From Danika's Casebook

Pet-assisted therapy is becoming more and more accepted by the mainstream medical establishment. Its benefits have been touted for many years—in fact, Florence Nightingale was a proponent of it—but pet-assisted therapy only has been put into actual practice in medical facilities in the past few decades. However, the results continue to show that humans simply feel better and heal faster when pets are included in their recovery. Perhaps it's the feeling of comfort, or the distraction from their own cares, or the unconditional acceptance and love that so many animals give. Whatever the reason, it causes humans to work harder at rehabilitation exercises, to focus longer on learning new skills, to build self-confidence and motivation in the face of seemingly insurmountable odds, and generally to speed their recovery and improve their lives in ways that many doctors may have thought impossible.

Mark This Spot!

If you think you and your dog would enjoy pet-assisted therapy work, there are a number of organizations that you can contact for guidance. Try these websites for starters: Therapy Dogs Inc. at **http://therapydogs.com** (no www.), Delta Society at **www.deltasociety.org/default.html**, and Therapy Dogs International at **www.tdi-dog.org**. These organizations are dedicated to developing and maintaining certification programs to ensure that all therapy dogs have a standard basic training. Many local therapy dog organizations are registered affiliates of these groups, and will require you and your dog to successfully complete their training.

This unexplainable bond that humans have with animals may continue to surprise and delight us with potential as yet unimaginable. As you work with your dog and build your communication skills, you may find many ways in which you can both add to each other's health and happiness!

Now that we've learned what our dogs can do for us, it's time to move on to a scary topic: What happens if our beloved pet is lost? Once again, you can add your telepathic abilities to the other resources you call on to find him. Let's turn the page and find out how.

Help! My Dog Is Lost!

"We had a lovable, mixed-breed mutt named Pal when I was a kid. Pal was very friendly—a pal to everyone he met. The first time he took off from the backyard of our city row home, we were frantic, sure that he'd quickly get lost among the look-alike neighborhoods or be hit by a car on one of the busy streets. We scoured the area, calling from the car, our bikes, or on foot. After a tense day had gone by, Pal showed up, obviously well fed and happy, and not in any way frightened or remorseful. He would disappear like this every couple of weeks, and eventually we found out that he had a regular circle of friends he would visit. They all were owners of some type of neighborhood establishment—the butcher, grocer, pizza place, etc. At first these folks thought he was lost and took pity on him, and then they looked forward to his visits as he made his rounds—he was the best-fed 'lost dog' there ever was!"

—Bud N.

There isn't anything much more terrifying than realizing that one of your loved ones is missing. There's a panic that overtakes you when you realize that he isn't where you expected, and it grows when you search farther and still can find no sign of him.

It's not one of the better experiences in life to look in the backyard and notice that the gate is open, and your lovable mutt is nowhere to be found. I hope you never have to experience that horrible feeling in the pit of your stomach that tells you that your dog is lost.

Although felines are acclaimed for their curiosity, I think it's safe to say that they haven't cornered the market. Dogs are fond of following their noses wherever they may lead them, and sometimes it's somewhere so interesting that they forget the way home. Some breeds, such as Siberian huskies and whippets, for example, are more prone than most to "exploring" something that catches their attention and losing their way home. Of course, curiosity is not the only reason dogs become lost: There are any number of other situations that end up with the same result, and none are particularly pleasant. However, some cases are more straightforward to solve than others.

For instance, if your pet has wandered off your property, it may be easier to locate him, because you have a good knowledge of the neighborhood and possible interesting spots. Often a dog on a "walkabout" will return on his own after his adventure—there are some dogs, like Pal at the beginning of this chapter, who consider themselves "neighborhood ambassadors" and feel it necessary to check out the locals once in a while.

Sometimes a traumatic incident at your home will cause your pet to run off: a fire or other emergency or a lightning storm that was frightening. It could be that your dog decided that that squirrel next door was so tempting it was worth the shock of the electric fence and made a run for it. If you have recently moved, the old house with its more familiar sights, smells, and sounds may prove to be too enticing. In these cases, you have a distinct area within which to begin your search.

In other cases, it can be much more difficult to locate your lost friend. For instance, he may have been thrown from the car during an accident or gotten loose while on a trip. The difficulty arises because you might be incapacitated yourself in the accident, or you may not be immediately aware of the fact that he's missing, and more time passes before the search begins. It's also more likely that both you and your dog are unfamiliar with the area, so deciding where to start, and what the logical progression should be, becomes more tricky.

Pawprint

Have you considered having a microchip inserted in your dog? In this simple procedure, a tiny microchip (about the size of a grain of rice) is placed beneath the skin between your dog's shoulder blades. Microchips are fairly inexpensive, and the manufacturers maintain a computerized database that allows instant identification when someone locates your pet. It's probably a good idea at any time, but if you are moving far from your current home or going on a long trip, you may want to give it more serious consideration.

Keep a Cool Head

Animal communication certainly can help you in this circumstance, but you must do your best to remain calm. In this instance, working with a friend may provide better information, simply because your friend is likely to be somewhat more emotionally detached from the situation.

Be aware that locating lost animals is a specialty within the realm of professional animal communication. Many animal communicators refuse to do lost-pet consultations. This is not out of heartlessness: it is partly because their clearer connection with animals tends to cause a higher level of emotional involvement, and some communicators are seriously affected until the animal is found.

Doing a consultation for someone whose beloved pet is lost is frequently a no-win situation for the communicator. Often both human and dog are so stressed that the information given and received is not clear. Also, a dog's perspective and descriptions are very different from a human's—the person may want to hear a street name, while the dog talks about interesting smells or scary sounds.

If the animal is injured, often the pain is transmitted not the location. Sometimes when an animal is unconscious there will be an ability to see from "above" the body, and at other times there may be a fuzzy, luminous feeling; both are virtually indistinguishable from the sensations transmitted by an animal who has crossed over. Because animals do not have the same fears about death, there may be a feeling of lightness or even happiness at having left the body (especially if they were injured or old and feeble). It can be difficult to distinguish the various feelings and give clear information about the dog's location and condition.

Then again, sometimes the animal simply does not want to be found. There are a number of reasons for this, and most are difficult for the owner to accept. Some dogs are nomads by nature, and they refuse to settle down permanently, staying with one family for a time and then moving on to another when the wanderlust strikes. Others will decide to leave a situation that does not suit them. Perhaps they live in an abusive household, or a new family member (human or animal) has arrived, or a favored companion has left or died, or they have their own reasons that we may not understand. Older dogs or those who are near death sometimes will leave because they prefer to die on their own terms, or they don't want to upset the family members by forcing a euthanasia decision.

As you can see, working with lost animals is fraught with pitfalls, even for the best of animal communicators. When you are trying to find your own lost pet, it can seem daunting, but you may be the best person for the task, because you already have a strong connection with the dog.

EXERCISE 10

Reaching Out to Your Lost Dog

Animal communication *can* help you find your pet. Here are some techniques to aid you in calling your lost friend home:

1. First, remain calm. You won't be able to accomplish anything if you are overly distraught.

2. Remember to visualize what you *want* your dog to do. Empty your mind of your fears, and remain as positive and optimistic as possible.

3. Use the Sacred Clearing visualization (page 37) to connect with your dog telepathically. Go inside to your safe space to ask questions about your dog's safety and condition, for as much information as possible about current surroundings, and for anything else that might clue you to where your dog is. Also ask why your dog left, if you don't know already. You also may ask if he *wants* to come home. Don't scold or make demands for a quick return—you may make the dog more upset.

4. While you are visualizing, you can use the same gold or silver cord technique I described on page 74 in Chapter 4 for calling your puppy to you. Simply visualize a beautiful cord attached to your heart that is reaching across the distance to your pet's heart.

Telepathically tell your dog that he can use this cord to come home to you.

5. If any information you received in Step 3 helps you recognize where your dog is, you may be able to guide him back to you—visualize walking from that location back to your home, using sensory clues that your dog would recognize (for example, fencing in front of a yard rather than a street sign or the smell of a honey-suckle bush instead of a house number).

6. If you have difficulty reaching your pet in the Sacred Clearing, do not automatically assume the worst. It simply may be due to the dog's stress over being lost or frightened or due to your own stress about the situation. Ask your Spirit Guide to help you (see page 39 for more on your Spirit Guide), as well as any other spiritual assistants you may have. Sometimes other household pets, even ones who already have crossed over, will be able to make contact with your dog and help bring him home.

KEEP TRYING

If you experience difficulty contacting your dog at first, take a break and try again later. This is a stressful time for you both, and persisting only may succeed in making you feel more anxious and therefore unable to receive communication clearly. Sometimes a short period of rest or quiet meditation will clear your mind, calm your nerves, and allow you to proceed with better results. If you have a friend who also knows animal communication, ask for help: Another set of senses may provide you with clues you haven't picked up on your own.

Receiving information that your dog is injured or unconscious may overly distress you. It is certainly difficult to feel your pet's pain and not be able to physically reach out to soothe the hurt. Remember that your telepathic communication may help locate the dog sooner so that medical attention can be provided; this knowledge should help you to keep your composure. Again, if you receive such information, don't hesitate to ask a friend for confirmation and assistance.

As I mentioned earlier, sometimes you will receive a fuzzy or light feeling that could indicate either unconsciousness or that the animal has crossed over. Because it can be difficult to tell, my tendency is to lean towards the former. That condition is changeable, so it is possible that later attempts at communication could yield clearer information. If the dog merely is unconscious, at some point you may be able to pick up details of the surrounding environment. If the dog indeed has crossed over, the fuzziness may change to a more definite feeling of detachment or even a clear message of the new state as the animal becomes aware of the change. Although this is never the message you would wish to receive, I believe it is better to know the true circumstances than to be left wondering.

EXERCISE 11

Dowsing

Another method that many animal communicators will use in addition to telepathic communication to help determine a lost pet's location is dowsing over a map. On page 78 in Chapter 4, I gave you instructions on how to use a pendulum to dowse for information to help you choose the right puppy or dog. I mentioned that you could dowse over a map to help you determine whether a particular breeder's location was where your new pup would come from. You can use this same map technique to help you locate your missing dog.

Start by using the largest-scale map you can find of the area where you think your dog may be lost. Using a pencil and ruler, divide the area into quadrants. Use the pendulum over each quadrant in succession, asking the question, "Is Sasha in this quadrant?" (insert your dog's name, of course). When you receive a "yes" answer, divide that section into quadrants, and repeat the process until you have as specific a location as possible. This works especially well if you have someone who can begin looking for your dog while you dowse. Or, alternately, you can look while a friend dowses, and you can keep in touch by cell phone as you narrow the search.

Doggie Diaries

One of the spiritual helpers I call on in my work as an animal communicator is a cat of mine who lived with me for fourteen years before crossing over. He was a good, sweet-natured tabby, who in many ways behaved more like a dog. Since he has been in spirit form, he has come to be known as "The Flying Tiger," and I call on him to help me with difficult cases.

One time I did a consultation for a friend whose schipperke, Bertie, had taken off one afternoon shortly after a new pet, a cat, was brought into the house. The owner was frantic, because she lived in a development that backed up to a major highway, with only one hundred feet of open space that was heavy with bushes and weeds between her home and the road.

Before I began, I called upon my Flying Tiger to help, because I was more emotionally involved with this case than usual—I knew Bertie well. I asked him to go out and locate the little dog and help her find her way home. Then I settled in to contact Bertie directly.

As I suspected, she was angry and jealous of the new household member, and she thought running away would "show them." However, once in the brushy area, she became disoriented and couldn't find her way back out, and this frightened her. I told her that her family was very upset that she had left, and that they loved her very much. The new cat had been abandoned and was starving when they took her in, and they had hoped that Bertie would befriend her and help her get back to health. I then told Bertie to look for the Flying Tiger, and he would lead her out of the brush and all the way home if she needed him to, since all the townhouses in her neighborhood looked the same from the backyard.

After several hours wandering around in the weeds in the dark, Bertie was ready to come home. Within an hour or so of speaking with me, she showed up on her doorstep, with bits of weeds and dirt in her fur but none the worse for wear and happy to be reunited with her family. Of course, I thanked my Flying Tiger for his help once again!

—From Danika's Casebook

Mark This Spot!

If your dog doesn't return quickly or was lost on vacation or during a move or accident, check Pets 911. They have a Web site (**www.Pets911.com**) and a toll-free, automated hotline (1-888-PETS-911) that allows you to search tens of thousands of lost-and-found pet listings from all areas of the United States. It includes information from some 950 animal shelters and adoption groups as well. You also can place your own "Lost" listing, including a photo. Also check the "Lost and Found" classified section out. If your dog has a microchip, notify your veterinarian or the manufacturer (whoever is the proper contact) immediately. Don't forget to check with your local shelters and police departments, call all the local veterinary hospitals, and put up signs and ads locally in groceries and other stores and gathering places—the more coverage the better!

Hopefully, the use of these techniques will result in the quick and safe return of your canine companion. Unfortunately, sometimes the outcome is not so joyous. If your pet is seriously injured or has crossed over, it can be devastating. Remember in these circumstances that your telepathic skills may help bring medical aid sooner or, at the very least, may have comforted your friend throughout the process of dying. Do not discount the value of this comfort to your pet.

I certainly hope that your animal communication skills need never be put to this use. But honing your skills with constant practice may prove to be the best means of reuniting you with your dog if he ever becomes lost. Even though the situation is incredibly stressful, when the outcome is the happy, safe return of your friend, it all will be worthwhile.

In the next chapter, we'll talk about what happens when your pet crosses over. As the experiences of many animal communicators attest, even when your beloved dog's earthly life is over, he will remain psychically connected to you.

Connecting in Heaven

"I lost Butterscotch, my collie/shepherd, several years ago. My faithful friend had epilepsy for the last three to four years of her short, nine-year life. About a week after her death, I had a dream, and in my dream Butterscotch came back to me in a vision. It was as if I was awake and she was coming toward me—it was as clear as day. It was as if she was saying 'It's okay, Mom, it's okay.'"

—Cheryl Minney

After spending an entire lifetime with a friend as faithful as a dog can be, it's extremely difficult for most of us to say good-bye. It certainly seems to be unfair that an animal that brings such happiness to us should have such a short life. However, the fact remains that, depending on the breed, the lifespan of dogs is eight to fifteen years, while that of humans in industrialized countries is in the mid-70s.

Facing the death of our loved ones is never easy; whether it's caused by illness, accident, or old age, we're never fully prepared for it. Even if we are aware of its eventuality or make the final decision for euthanasia to relieve suffering, the stark and suddenly empty spot in our household and the hole it leaves in our hearts can be overwhelming. This is one of the great dilemmas of choosing to live with pets that don't outlive you: The joy of their company is counterbalanced by the shortness of their lives. In my opinion, the joy far outweighs the heartache.

What Dogs Teach Us

Some of the greatest lessons dogs have for us are tied to this very issue. First among them is to enjoy every minute you have. Dogs are great at living in the present moment. They put everything into each experience, whether it's chasing a ball, licking your face, enjoying a meal, or lying in the sun. When they're happy, they are ecstatic, and they're not worrying about when it will end. Even when something doesn't go right, or they don't feel well, they don't latch onto it and nurture the difficulties—as soon as they're able, they go back to having a good time.

This is another valuable lesson: Don't hold onto problems or bad experiences. Just let them go. Life is too short to waste on the negative stuff. Perhaps our longer lives give us the impression that we've got more time to "fix things later," even though holding grudges or focusing on our worries only causes more problems for us. Dogs seem to have an innate ability to forgive and forget very quickly, and it's a skill we should all take heed and learn.

Another lesson that canines have for us is that of acceptance of death. I have communicated with many dogs who are about to cross over or who already have, and one theme is consistent: that death is not to be feared. It's a natural part of life, and it is akin to taking off one coat and putting on another. If I didn't believe in reincarnation before I communicated with the animals, I certainly was convinced of it by them!

Of all the dogs I have spoken with who were nearing death, only two expressed any fear of it. In both cases, euthanasia was being considered prematurely, and the dogs subsequently recovered from their illnesses. Every other dog assured me that there was no fear attached to crossing over. In fact, some were very tired of dealing with their chronic illnesses and looked forward to finding new, healthier bodies. To be honest, their greatest apprehension stemmed from their feelings for their humans—they did not want to cause them pain or sadness, or they did not want to leave them alone. Some pets have hung onto life long after they would have chosen to leave simply because they knew their owners weren't ready for them to die, and they didn't want to be the cause of such distress.

Often these dogs instinctively know that their owners would feel so guilty about choosing euthanasia or would be emotionally unable to handle witnessing the death, so they arrange to depart when the owner is away or unavailable. I have had a number of people tell me that although they kept close watch on their ailing friend, he crossed over when they were not around, even if they had left for only a short period of time. I consider this to be a last gift from a lifelong friend who understands us better than we understand ourselves.

Doggie Diaries

Over a period of time, I worked with a client who had an eight-year-old fox terrier named Grady who had numerous health issues. Grady was a warmhearted dog who felt that it was his job to be a steady companion and source of emotional support for his owner and to serve as protector for her and her family.

Grady had Cushing's disease, which affects the adrenal glands and produces symptoms that mimic diabetes and other serious disorders. In addition, he had cataracts that continued to worsen. Although he was not a miserable dog, his quality of life was beginning to deteriorate. Grady's owner, a wonderful, caring woman, was as devoted to him as he was to her. She spent many hours and dollars on Grady's health and welfare, and the next step was to be surgery to remove the cataracts.

Grady was looking forward to the operation very much, even though it would cause discomfort at first. This was mainly due to the fact that the cataracts had progressed to the point where he was almost blind, and he felt he could no longer perform his job, because he was constantly bumping into things. When I asked how he felt about having the operation done, he kept saying, "I want to see! I want to see!"

About two weeks before the cataract operation was scheduled to take place, Grady contracted a mysterious set of symptoms that caused his owner to take him to the emergency vet. He had ulcers in his mouth and throat, and he refused to eat. No obvious reasons for the symptoms could be found other than possible ingestion of a caustic material or contact with another infected dog who showed no symptoms. Unfortunately, because Grady's immune system was already weakened, within a week, his condition worsened to the point that he was near death.

Because he was at an emergency vet who was more than ninety minutes from home, his owner was not able to be with him when he crossed over. She was so distraught when she called me one final time to tell me that Grady was gone; she said she felt so guilty for not being there for him at the end.

When I tapped into Grady's spirit, the first thing he said was, "I can see! I can see!" He also indicated that although he had been looking forward to the cataract operation, the most recent illness was just more than he could take. It had taken him by surprise, and he was simply tired of dealing with his poor health and felt it was time to move on. He felt that with all his medical problems, he was becoming too large a burden for his owner, whose husband also was chronically ill. He wasn't able to be helpful to her the way he had been before, and he found it very undignified to be constantly bumping into things.

Grady also made it clear that although he at first hoped that his owner would be with him at the vet's, when he realized that it wasn't possible at that moment, he quickly decided to move on anyway and was not angry or upset at all. He clearly did not want his owner to feel guilty. He loved her very much, and he appreciated everything she'd done for him. In fact, he would continue to be with her in spirit for a while; he was in no hurry to reincarnate, because he wanted to be sure he found a healthy body this time. Grady indicated that he would come back to her, but that it might not be for a few months or possibly a year, and he might decide to come back to her as a one- or two-year-old dog not as a puppy.

Grady's owner, while sad for her loss, was happy that he could see again and was comforted by the news that he would still be with her in spirit and would come back at some point in the future. She had already felt his presence in the house several times, and she plans to use the Sacred Clearing visualization to maintain contact with her beloved friend.

—*From Danika's Casebook*

Moving On

Moving on is something that dogs and other animals do very well. As I've said, the analogy I've been given time and time again is that death is merely taking off one coat and putting on another. If a dog has been chronically ill for a long time or is advanced in age, moving on to the next life often is welcomed. It's a chance to leave behind the old, worn-out body and to spend some time gathering energy while selecting a new body and a new life.

GRIEVING

When any loved one has departed, there is a period of mourning in which we deal with the grief caused by their loss. I think it is important to allow some time for sadness; without it, I don't think we ever really heal from the loss. Even up until the early 20th century, it was common for people to mourn family members for a full year. Now, however, it seems that we expect mourners to be back to normal within a few days or a couple of weeks.

I also have come across people who think it's silly to grieve over the loss of a pet, which is such a shame. If you think about it, our pets often spend more time with us than other family members, and they are frequently greater sources of support and comfort. This is especially true for single and elderly people whose pets are their family. It seems to me that it's only natural that there is sadness at the empty space left by a pet's death—it's a recognition of that close bond we shared.

In my opinion, you should have whatever type of memorial for your dog that best suits you. Pay tribute to your dog's love and friendship in a way that seems fitting to you, and don't let someone else make you feel foolish or talk you out of it—you will regret it later. There are many ways to memorialize your pet, from a simple burial at home (if permitted by local laws) to a full-fledged funeral at a pet cemetery. Only you can decide what feels right for you and your family.

It's normal to want to keep collars, toys, dishes, and even a bit of fur or your pet's ashes; after all, this was a family member. As time passes, you may find that you don't need to keep everything but only a special item or two. Photos are also helpful to remember your friend and can be very comforting in your grief.

Allow yourself to go through the steps of the grieving process on your own schedule; there is no right way, there is only *your* way. It is important to remember that it will take some time to move on from these feelings. Don't rush your grieving, and don't be afraid to get help.

Mark This Spot!

There are many resources that are available for grieving pet owners—from books to workshops to consultations with a therapist. The following are two comprehensive Web sites and a hotline that you may find helpful:

800-404-PETS, a toll-free, 24-hour pet grief support line.

Association for Pet Loss and Bereavement, a nonprofit, worldwide clearinghouse for information on grieving the loss of a pet. (**www.aplb.org**)

Pet Loss Grief Support Web site, a site with resources, a chat room, and a community environment for grieving owners. (**www.petloss.com**)

Making Room to Grieve

When a beloved pet dies, we can be so wrapped up in our own grieving that we forget that there are others who feel the loss as well. Other family members, especially children, will need their own time to grieve and may need some assistance in understanding what has happened, as well as dealing with the impact on their daily lives.

Be cautious about simply replacing the recently deceased dog with a new puppy; this has some negative connotations for both you and your children. For instance, it may avert attention from your sadness, but it also inhibits you and your children from expressing grief in the present and prevents you from giving your feelings healthy attention now. Something else to consider is that repressed grief has been shown to cause a number of illnesses—it eventually resurfaces one way or another.

Such avoidance may also send your children the message that grief is not acceptable, which could be harmful to their emotional well-being later in life. It also does not recognize the pet's importance as a family member, and it may imply that animals are not significant enough to grieve over. It implies that when one "breaks," you simply buy another one to replace it. I find this attitude that animals are "things" particularly repugnant and disrespectful of the love and friendship that our animal companions give us.

If you have other pets in the household, you may find a distinct change in demeanor as they, too, mourn their loss. Now that you have experience communicating with your dog, this should not come as a surprise. Be aware that each animal will have a unique response, just as humans express their grief individually.

Doggie Diaries

I once had the great privilege of working with Vic, a wonderful Shih tzu. One of Vic's owners regrettably decided to commit suicide and did so while Vic was the only one home. Not only did Vic stay with her the whole time, but he protected her body until she was found the next day. In his heartbreaking conversation with me about it, he kept indicating that he felt responsible, and that he wished he could have done something more to help her. I told him that he gave her the best gift of all: a friend to stand by her and be there with her to the end. Vic always has been a perfect example for me of the kind of true loyalty only a dog can give.

—From Danika's Casebook

My pal Joshua, the lovable Siberian husky, for example, was absolutely desolate when his beloved mate of five years, Seva, crossed over. He was lonely, depressed, and inconsolable for several months until a new friend came to the household, a beautiful female Samoyed named Aliya. She has helped Josh recover from his grief, and they have become a devoted couple.

The point is to realize that others in the family will be affected by the passing of your dog. In some cases, the animal members may feel the pain even more acutely than you, simply because they may have spent all of their time with the departed. However, they have fewer ways to show the extent of their grief. This is a prime opportunity to use your animal communication skills to help them through their mourning process and alleviate their pain. You'll probably find that supporting your other family members—furry and otherwise—will help you heal as well.

CONNECTING ACROSS THE RAINBOW BRIDGE

You can maintain contact with your departed dog by using the same communication techniques you have been using all along. The spirit is what you spoke to before, and that is what "crosses over"—nothing has changed except the physical form. The spirit merely has unzipped a costume and stepped out of it and is now searching the wardrobe for the next one to put on.

I suggest using the Sacred Clearing visualization to meet with your dog during this time of distress. Follow the same steps you've used during your dog's life to connect telepathically with him. This also is an excellent time to use the golden cord visualization to maintain your heart connection with your dog. (The Sacred Clearing and golden cord visualizations are described on pages 37 and 78 in Chapters 2 and 4.)

Depending on the circumstances of your dog's death, contacting him immediately after crossing over may not yield a lot of information. First of all, you may be so upset by your loss that you are unable to clearly pick up your dog's thoughts or feelings. In addition, if your pet departed quickly and unexpectedly, such as in a car accident, he still may be confused about where he is and may not even know he's left his body.

Your dog may also enjoy the new feeling of being disconnected from his body and may transmit nothing more than a light, floating feeling or an incoherent fuzziness. This is especially likely if he had serious or chronic health issues, was unconscious before death, or was frightened or in pain just before crossing. Don't be discouraged; wait a little while and try again. In the meantime, keep your mind and heart open to receiving messages in other forms. You may experience other signs or phenomena more clearly than telepathic messages at first. As an example, read the story of Bonnie and Kathleen below.

Doggie Diaries

Bonnie was my beautiful, sweet, loving Shetland sheepdog. When she was eleven years old, she developed bladder cancer. I tried various methods of treatment for her to no avail.

When she stopped wanting to eat, I knew the time had come for me to let her go. While we were in the examining room, waiting for the vet to come in and end her suffering, I kept talking to her, telling her how much I loved her, and asking her to please let me know, after she crossed, that she was okay.

During this time, she never stopped staring at me. I felt that she was trying to burn my image into her mind. There were times when neither of us said anything, we just stared at each other. It was such a sad time, but I could feel the love flowing between us. This went on for about ten minutes. Then the vet came in, administered the needle, and my little dog that I loved so much died.

Later that afternoon, I was sitting at my kitchen table having a cup of coffee. I was thinking about Bonnie and how much I was going to miss her. I was hoping that she was okay.

Unexpectedly, one of the seven recessed lights I have in my kitchen went out, and then came back on. This light never did this before, hasn't done it since, and in the two years since Bonnie's death, has yet to need replacing.

I know that Bonnie was telling me she was fine, and she was with me.

—*Kathleen R. Fisher*

As you can see, messages may come in an unexpected form. Your dog may choose to communicate with you in any number of ways and also may pick something that's especially meaningful for you both. For example, if you jingled your keys each time you prepared to take your dog for a walk, you might occasionally hear keys jingling, or your key ring might mysteriously jump off its hook—this may be an indication that your dog is thinking of you or is nearby. The physical ability to bark or jump up on you may be gone, but the spirit will find a way to be heard. I encourage you to adopt the same attitude as when you first started communicating telepathically: Believe that what you receive is real, without editing or second-guessing the form or content.

WHAT'S NEXT?

When I speak with a client whose dog has recently crossed over, the questions I am asked most frequently is, "Is my dog coming back to me?" and "When will he or she come back?"

For those who believe, as I do, that reincarnation is a reality, it is hard not to want a quick answer to these questions. Unfortunately, this usually is not as easy as we'd like. I do not claim to be an expert in this field by any means; however, it seems that there are a number of factors determining when, how, and whether a being will reincarnate.

The animals I have spoken with give answers ranging from "I don't know" to a specific time frame and the breed type of the future body. My experience tells me that each being and circumstance is unique, so there are no quick, easy answers to these questions.

Some dogs are particularly attached to their owners and feel a responsibility to remain with them even in spirit form—they don't want to take the chance of reincarnating and ending up with some-one else. In this case, the owners often will say that they can feel the dog's presence in the house or experience instances of seeing the dog's form or hearing the bark.

Other dogs want to reincarnate quickly and return to the same family, and they may find a way to do so. I have spoken with some dogs who expressed an interest in changing species—for example, one dog who grew up with cats thought they had more freedom and decided that next time she'd come back as a feline.

I also have spoken with dogs who were previously human and chose to come back as a dog because they wanted to be with a particular family member but didn't want to take the time to go through the longer human childhood. (Remember what I said about speciesism in Chapter 2—I've had too many animals tell me that they are reincarnated humans to believe that it's not possible, or that it is somehow a step "backward." It appears to me that embodied experience is just that—experience—and that there are lessons to be learned no matter what form it takes.)

When you are visiting with your dog in the Sacred Clearing, ask your questions about when and whether the spirit will return to a body. You also may want to ask what your pet will look like and how you will recognize him next time. These answers may not come right away, so don't be discouraged. Some animals may choose to stay in spirit for a time or even permanently. Others look forward to reincarnating immediately, and still others may be very particular about finding just the "right" body or experience to return to. You may want to check in with your dog at the Sacred Clearing every once in a while to see whether a new body has presented itself and your friend is ready to share the information.

Keep in mind that there's nothing wrong with stating your wish to be with your friend again, as long as you don't tie the spirit to you so tightly that it becomes a constricting bind rather than a loving connection. Remember that your pet has his own path, and if you cling to the past, you'll only make it more difficult for your friend to move on. It's better for you both to let go with love and hope that your paths will cross again.

Another possibility for seeing your friend again is as a "walk-in." Sometimes an animal will make an agreement to share or take over a body of another animal, either temporarily or permanently. Perhaps the host is dissatisfied with the living situation or the body and is looking for a way out. This phenomenon also occurs sometimes in multipet households. For a period of time after the death of a pet, its spirit may not be ready to move on, and it hangs around the familiar environment, occasionally appearing in spirit form or inhabiting the body of one of the other pets.

You may notice a marked change in the behavior or personality of one of your pets when this happens: They may act exactly like the recently deceased dog. In fact, you may catch yourself using the wrong name, thinking that you've just seen your departed friend, and you probably have. Often these episodes will taper off as the dog makes the transition and moves on. Sometimes, however, the dog opts to stay with the family in spirit form, choosing not to reincarnate.

I know that some people may find these events disturbing, but I find them comforting. I have no fear of the spirits of my deceased pets. They loved me in life; why would that change after death? It is wonderful to catch a glimpse out of the corner of my eye or suddenly feel a presence in a familiar spot on the couch—it makes me feel warm and happy that my friend still thinks of me and wants to be around me.

Sometimes it seems that dogs don't *need* to live as long as humans do: They've already learned the most important lessons! And isn't it wonderful that they've chosen to share their lives and wisdom with us?

Resources and Recommended Reading

INTRODUCTION

Brandenburg, Jim. *Brother Wolf: A Forgotten Promise*. Minocqua, WI: North Word Press, Inc., 1993.

Carter, Forrest. *The Education of Little Tree*. Albuquerque: University of New Mexico Press, 1976.

Curtis, Anita. *How to Hear the Animals*. Gilbertsville, PA: Anita Curtis, 1998. www.anitacurtis.com.

Farley, Walter. *The Black Stallion* Series. New York: Random House.

Fitzpatrick, Sonya. *The Pet Psychic*. www.sonyafitzpatrick.com.

Hill, Ruth Beebe. *Hanta Yo*. New York: Warner Books, 1979.

King, Serge Kahili, PhD *Urban Shaman: A Handbook for Personal and Planetary Transformation Based on the Hawaiian Way of the Adventurer*. New York: Fireside, 1990.

The Pet Psychic (television show starring Sonya Fitzpatrick), Animal Planet Television, animal.discovery.com.

Smith, Penelope. *Animal Talk: Interspecies Telepathic Communication*. Point Reyes, CA: Pegasus Publications, 1989. www.animaltalk.net.

Steinbeck, John. *Travels with Charley*. New York: The Viking Press, 1962.

Wenger, Cindy. Animal Communicator. www.PeaceableKingdomAC.com.

White, E.B. *Charlotte's Web*. New York: Harper & Row, 1952.

CHAPTER 1

Boone, J. Allen. *Kinship with All Life*. New York: Harper & Row, 1954.

Brandenburg, Jim. *Brother Wolf: A Forgotten Promise*. Minocqua, WI: North Word Press, Inc., 1993.

Brunke, Dawn Baumann. *Animal Voices*. Rochester, VT: Bear & Company, 2002.

Sheldrake, Rupert, PhD *Seven Experiments that Could Change the World: A Do-It-Yourself Guide to Revolutionary Science*. 2nd ed. Rochester, VT: Park Street Press, 2002

_____. *Dogs that Know When Their Owners are Coming Home, and Other Unexplained Powers of Animals*. New York: Crown Publishers, 1999.

_____. *The Sense of Being Stared At and Other Aspects of the Extended Mind*. New York: Crown Publishers, 2003.

Rupert Sheldrake's Web site for information about experiments and sharing of data, as well as other books and videos: **www.sheldrake.org**.

CHAPTER 2

Andrews, Ted. *Animal Speak: The Spiritual & Magical Powers of Creatures Great & Small*. St. Paul, MN: Llewellyn Publications, 1998.

Hill, Napoleon. *Think and Grow Rich*. reissue edition. New York: Ballantine Books, 1987.

King, Serge Kahili, PhD *Urban Shaman: A Handbook for Personal and Planetary Transformation Based on the Hawaiian Way of the Adventurer*. New York: Fireside, 1990.

Rood, Ronald. *Animals Nobody Loves*. Shelburne, VT: The New England Press, 1971.

Schweitzer, Albert. "Reverence for Life," Chapter 26 of *The Philosophy of Civilization*. New York: The MacMillan Company, 1949.

CHAPTER 3

Andersen, Jodi. *The Latchkey Dog, How the Way You Live Shapes the Behavior of the Dog You Love*. New York: HarperCollins Publishers, 2000.

The Dog Whisperer with Cesar Millan (television show), National Geographic Television.

Millan, Cesar. Dog Psychology Center of LA, 919 E. 61st St., Los Angeles, CA 90001. **www.dogpsychologycenter.com**, workshops, video.

Chapter 4

American Pet Products Manufacturers Association (APPMA) 2003–2004 National Pet Owners Survey.

The Humane Society of the United States. **www.hsus.org**.

iVillage. Dog information page. **www.ivillage/pets/dogs**.

How to Love Your Dog: A Kids Guide to Dog Care. **http://loveyourdog.com**.

Pedigree Brand. Mars Incorporated. **www.pedigree.com**.

Petfinder Web site to adopt a homeless pet: **www.petfinder.com**.

Pets 911. **www.Pets911.com**.

Call toll-free automated hotline at 1-888-PETS-911.

Chapter 5

Wright, John C., DVM, and Judi Wright Lashnits. A*in't Misbehavin'*. Emmaus, PA: Rodale Press, 2001.

Chapter 6

Bergin, Bonnie, EdD. *Understanding "Dog Mind."* Boston: Little, Brown and Company, 2000.

Canine Companions for Independence. Santa Rosa, CA. 707-577-1700. **www.caninecompanions.org**.

King, Serge Kahili, PhD *Urban Shaman: A Handbook for Personal and Planetary Transformation Based on the Hawaiian Way of the Adventurer.* New York: Fireside, 1990.

Chapter 7

Coren, Stanley. *How to Speak Dog.* New York: The Free Press, 2000.

Dibra, Bash. *Dog Speak.* New York: Simon & Schuster, 1999.

Editors of *Pets: Part of the Family* magazine. *Pet Speak.* Emmaus, PA: Rodale Inc., 2000.

Owens, Paul. *The Dog Whisperer: A Compassionate, Nonviolent Approach to Dog Training.* Holbrook, MA: Adams Media Corporation, 1999.

The Association of Pet Dog Trainers. Greenville, SC. 1-800-PET-DOGS. **www.apdt.com**

CHAPTER 8

Books

Bach, Edward, MD, and F.J. Wheeler, MD. *Bach Flower Remedies*. New York: Keats Publishing, 1952.

David, Kathy Diamond. *Therapy Dogs: Training Your Dog to Reach Others*. New York: Howell Book House, 1992.

Travel Information and Destinations

Coyote Communications. **www.coyote communications.com/dogcamp.html.** (dog camping information)

Dog Scouts of America (DSA). **www.dogscouts.com.**

Door to Summer. **www.doortosummer.com /door/civic/ petintusa.htm.** (pet-friendly locations)

Four Paws Kingdom. Rutherfordton, NC. 828-287-7324. **www.4pawskingdom.com**

www.HappyDogTravel.com.

Kind Planet. Creston, CA. 805-277-0205. **www.KindPlanet.org/travel.html**

Travel Reservation Web Sites

Bring Your Pet
www.BringYourPet.com

Companion Air
www.CompanionAir.com

Cruise America RVs **www.CruiseAmerica.com**

Dog Paddling Adventures **www.DogPaddlingAdventures.com** (canoe trips in Canada)

Go RVing: **www.GoRVing.com**

Private Motor Home Rentals **www.MotorHomeRental.ws**

Pets Welcome: **www.PetsWelcome.com**

Travel Product Web Sites

Cool Dog Products **www.CoolDogProducts.com**

Dog Logic: **www.DogLogic.com** (dog information and products)

Drs. Foster & Smith, Inc **www.DrsFosterSmith.com**

TailsbytheLake.com **www.TailsByTheLake.com**

Other Resources

www.DogsWithJobs.com (Web site for *Dogs with Jobs* television show)

Chapter 9

About.com. **http://dogs.about.com.**
Type "mental health" in the search box on the home page.
American Holistic Veterinary Association. Belair, MD. 410-569-0795.
www.ahvma.org
American Veterinary Chiropractic Assoc-iation. Bluejacket, OK. 918-784-2231. **www.animalchiropractic.org/**
International Veterinary Acupuncture Society. Ft. Collins, CO.
970-266-0666. **www.ivas.org**

Chapter 10

The American Journal of Cardiology. Elsevier Science. www.elsevier.com
Dogs with Jobs. Cineflix Productions, Inc. **www.dogswithjobs.com** (the *Dogs with Jobs* links page has a long list of pet organizations, including those that train and provide health or service dogs)
"Providing for your pet's future without you." The Humane Society of the United States. Washington, DC. 202-452-1100. **www.hsus.org**
Journal of the American Geriatrics Society. Blackwell Publishing.
www.blackwellpublishing.com
Journal of the American Medical Association (JAMA). American Medical Association. **www.jama.ama-assn.org/**
Lancet. Elsevier Limited. **www.thelancet.com/**
Psychiatric Service Dog Society. Arlington, VA. 571-216-1589.
www.psychdog.org/
Swedish Medical Center. Seattle. **www.swedish.org/15309.cfm**
Wheely Willy and Friends.
www.wheelywilly.com

Chapter 11

Pets 911: **www.Pets911.com,**
1-888-PETS-911

Chapter 12

800-404-PETS (toll-free, 24-hour pet grief support line)
Association for Pet Loss and Bereavement. **www.aplb.org** (a nonprofit world-wide clearinghouse for information about grieving the loss of a pet)
Pet Loss Grief Support Web site. **www.petloss.com** (a Web site with resources, a chat room, and a community environment for grieving owners)

Other Resources

Becker, Marty, Dr. *The Healing Power of Pets: Harnessing the Amazing Ability of Pets to Make and Keep People Happy and Healthy.* New York: Hyperion, 2002.

Bonnie Bergin's Training Camp (VHS). Edited from the KQED public television series *You and Your Great Dog,* 1996.

Davis, Kathy Diamond. *Therapy Dogs: Training Your Dog to Help Others,* 2d. ed. Wenatchee, WA: Dogwise Publishing, 2002.

Martin, Ann N. *Food Pets Die For: Shocking Facts About Pet Food.* Troutdale, OR: New Sage Press, 1997.

McElroy, Susan Chernak. *Animals as Teachers and Healers.* New York: Ballantine, 1997.

People Training for Dogs (DVD), Cesar Millan, Inc., 2005.

Raise with Praise (VHS), Burbank, CA: Raise with Praise, Inc., 1997.

Randolph, Mary. *Dog Law, 4th Ed.* Berkeley, CA: Nolo, 2001.

Reynolds, Rita M. *Blessing the Bridge: What Animals Teach Us About Death, Dying, and Beyond.* Troutdale, OR: New Sage Press, 2001.

Schultze, Kymythy R., CCN, AHI *Natural Nutrition for Dogs and Cats— The Ultimate Diet.* Carlsbad, CA: Hay House, 1999.

Volhard, Jack and Wendy. *The Canine Good Citizen: Every Dog Can Be One, 2d. Ed.* New York: Howell Book House, Hungry Minds, Inc., 1997.

The Whole Dog Journal, Greenwich, CT: Belvoir Publications. (A monthly guide to natural dog care and training.)

Other Web Site Resources

AKC Canine Good Citizen, **www.akc.org/events/cgc/index.cfm**

American Dog Trainers Network. **www.canine.org**

The Animal Rescue Site, (Help feed homeless animals by clicking daily for free!) **www.theanimalrescuesite.com.**

Assistance Dogs of America. **www.adai.org**

Carting with Your Dog.
www.cartingwithyourdog.com

Delta Society. **www.deltasociety.org** (international organization providing information and training for therapy and service animals and their trainers)

Dog Breed Information.
www.dogbreedinfo.com

Dogs with Disabilities.
www.dogdisability.com (for people with dogs who have special challenges)

Enota Mountain Retreat and Eco-spiritual Village, (Pet friendly camping, animal sanctuary, eco-spiritual lifestyle.) **www.enota.com and enota.org.**

For Pits' Sake. **www.forpitssake.org** (using American pit bull terriers in safety and educational programs)

Guiding Eyes for the Blind.
www.guiding-eyes.org

Homevet Natural Pet Care: Your Pet's Home for Holistic Healing, with Dr. Jeff Feinman, CVH. **www.homevet.com**

Paws With a Cause.
www.pawswithacause.org
(assistance dog training)

The Pet Professor. **www.thepetprofessor.com**

Therapy Dogs, Inc. **www.therapydogs.com**

Train Rite. **www.trainrite.org**
(trains shelter dogs as assistance dogs)

Working Dogs. **www.workingdogs.com** (information about working dogs)

Animal Organizations

American Anti-Vivisection Society
801 Old York Road, #204
Jenkintown, PA 19046
215-887-0816
1-800-SAY-AAVS
www.aavs.org

American Human Association
63 Inverness Drive East
Englewood, CO 80112
303-792-9900
www.americanhumane.org

Best Friends Animal Society
5001 Angel Canyon Road
Kanab, Utah 84741-5000
435-644-2001
www.bestfriends.org

**Bonnie Bergin's Assistance
Dog Institute**
1215 Sebastopol Road
Santa Rosa, CA 95407
707-545-DOGS
www.assistancedog.org

Defenders of Wildlife
National Headquarters
1130 17th Street, NW
Washington, DC 20036
202-682-9400
www.defenders.org

Doris Day Animal League
*(Working to reduce the pain and
suffering of non-human animals
through legislative initiatives.)*
227 Massachusetts Ave.,
NE, Suite 100
Washington, DC 20002
202-546-1761
www.ddal.org

The Farm Sanctuary
P.O. Box 150
Watkins Glen, NY 14891
607-583-2225
www.farmsanctuary.org

Humane Society of the United States
2100 L St., NW
Washington, DC 20037
202-452-1100
www.hsus.org

**International Fund for
Animal Welfare**
International Headquarters
411 Main Street
P.O. Box 193
Yarmouth Port, MA 02675
508-744-2000
www.ifaw.org

**The Latham Foundation for the
Promotion of Humane Education**
Latham Plaza Building
1826 Clement Avenue
Alameda, CA 94501
510-521-0920
www.latham.org

**People for the Ethical
Treatment of Animals**
501 Front Street
Norfolk, VA 23510
757-622-PETA
www.peta.org

**Society for the Prevention of
Cruelty to Animals**
424 E. 92nd St
New York, NY 10128-6804
212-876-7700
www.aspca.org

Therapy Dogs Inc.
P.O. Box 5868
Cheyenne, WY 82003
307-432-0272
http://therapydogs.com

Therapy Dogs International
88 Bartley Road
Flanders, NJ 07836
973-252-9800
www.tdi-dog.org

There also are many very good
local organizations working to help
animals! Please check your local
phone book, pet supply store, or
veterinarian for information, and
search online for an upcoming
Pet Expo in your area.

For a list of local animal shelters
and rescues, check your local phone
book, or go to **www.PetFinder.com**,
and click on the "Shelters &
Rescues" tab at the top.

About the Author

Danika Nadzan is an animal communicator and writer. She has ten years of experience helping clients understand what their pets are trying to tell them. She lives in Quakertown, Pennsylvania.